ADDICTED TO DYSFUNCTION

Released To Live Life Out Loud!

ADDICTED
TO
DYSFUNCTION

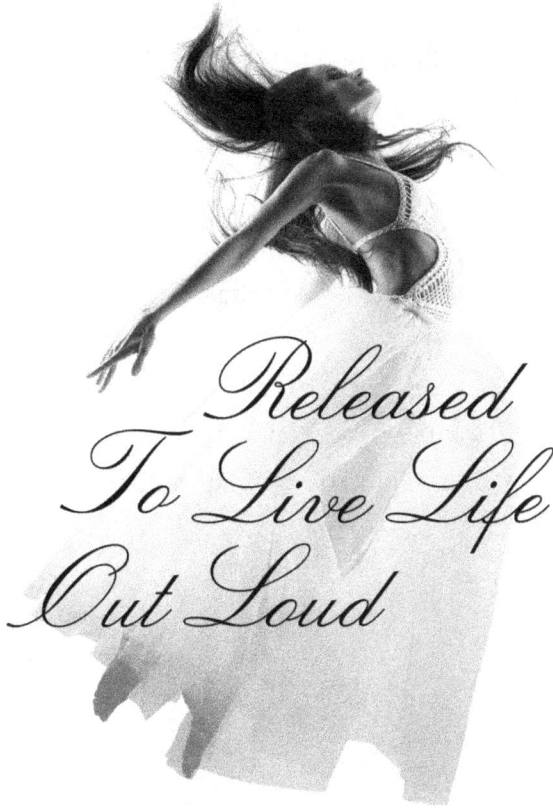

*Released
To Live Life
Out Loud*

BENITA TYLER

Published by:
Beloved Daffodil's Inspirations

Copyright © 2012 by (Benita Tyler)

ISBN: 978-0-9856964-0-5 Hard Cover Book
ISBN: 978-0-9856964-1-2 Paper Back
ISBN: 978-0-9856964-2-9 E-Book

First Edition, 2012
Published in the United States of America

Beloved Daffodil's Inspirations
P.O. Box 6395, Kokomo, Indiana 46904
www.BelovedDaffodilsInspirations.com

This book is dedicated to my beautiful mother Ann Benn. From her I get my ambition, strong will, and independence.

Acknowledgements

I share this book with my family: I thank my husband Cedric Tyler for his loving support, my oldest daughter who is my rock, and my sons & youngest daughter who I love unconditionally. Special dedications to the people who came to teach me life lessons: *job well done.* Special thanks to my spiritual advisor, Winged One — Thank you for your never-failing love and guidance. Thanks to Ty Gray for his friendship and guidance. Thank You Heavenly Father for Your love and protection. Blessings~

Contents

Chapter 1   A Child is Born - Life Lessons .1

Chapter 2   Disappointment: What a Father Brings 7

Chapter 3   Choices: A Boyfriend's Generosity 11

Chapter 4   Disappointment: Daddy, I'm Disappointed 13

Chapter 5   Choices: A Boyfriend from Hell! 19

Chapter 6   A Teenager's Transformation 25

Chapter 7   Those Awesome High School Years 31

Chapter 8   Forgiveness: A First Love's Impact 35

Chapter 9   Forgiveness: Just Ask For It 39

Chapter 10 Forgiveness: My Deepest Regret 43

Chapter 11 Awareness: Warning, Marriage Can be Hard 51

Chapter 12 Awareness: Chaos in the Streets 57

Chapter 13 Awareness: Dreams Fading Fast 61

Chapter 14 Awareness: Pack Up! It's Time to Go! 67

Chapter 15 Awareness: Left Without a Place to Go 73

Chapter 16 Awareness: The Twins Who Changed My Life 77

Chapter 17   Awareness: Why Does Marriage Have to be so Hard?.81

Chapter 18   Awareness: D.O.A on a Harlem Sidewalk 85

Chapter 19   Awareness: Running Out of Time. 91

Chapter 20   Awareness: A Widow's Survival. 95

Chapter 21   Awareness: New Beginnings in the Lone Star State . .99

Chapter 22   Awareness: Soldiers in Disguises. 103

Chapter 23   Acceptance:Heightened Hottie Alert 107

Chapter 24   Acceptance: Baggage (The What, Who,
              When, Where, & How). 111

Chapter 25   Acceptance: It's Official — I'm His. 121

Chapter 26   Acceptance: Children in Distress 127

Chapter 27   Acceptance: Raising Children Can Be Hard 139

Chapter 28   Acceptance: Following The Voice of God 143

Chapter 29   Acceptance:A Mother's Return 155

Chapter 30   Disappointment: Farewell to a Father 167

Chapter 31   Acceptance: Tension Everywhere 171

Chapter 32   Acceptance: An Accident Can Bring Awareness 181

Chapter 33   Forgiveness: Just Stopping By 189

Chapter 34   Acceptance: Putting the Pieces Back Together 201

Chapter 35   Close the Door and Don't Look Back!. 205

Chapter 36   Released to Live Life Out Loud. 213

*"I may not have gone where I intended to go,
but I think I have ended up where
I needed to be."*

– Douglas Adam

Respect

Who is this young girl? A "*beloved*" child of God left alone in the world, abandoned by the men who loved her most. Throughout the chapters of this young girl's life, she faced her demons. Many of them plagued her both mentally and emotionally. This young girl was part of the walking wounded stuck in life, who found herself *Addicted To Dysfunction*. This young girl's addiction nearly destroyed her. However, God never left her side. He sustained her throughout her life's journey, rebirthing her back to the woman she was meant to be. This young girl was released: to live life out loud. *That young girl is me!* So what if I'm fifty years old? That just means I'm not ashamed to tell you the naked truth — self-loathing, depression, suicidal thoughts, murder, and anger were just the tip of the iceberg as I transitioned though life learning new lessons. Perhaps it was all a cry for help and no one listened. It is even more likely that I was simply *Addicted To Dysfunction*.

CHAPTER 1

A Child is Born - Life Lessons

I was born in St. Louis, Missouri in July of 1961. God entrusted my parents to be the lucky contributors of the 23 chromosomes each that make me the unique individual that I am. My father was thirteen years older than my mother, having deceived her about his real age when they started dating. My father's brother was a friend of the family who rented an apartment in my great grandmother's multiple-family dwelling where my grandfather and my mother also resided. My father often visited his brother, which was how he met my mother. He was well liked by my mother's family, especially her aunts who adored him. They thought he was the perfect gentlemen and believed that he was a good suitor for my mother. My Aunt Zepherine would say, "Now, that's a fine-looking man, Ann."

My mother would be happy that she had their approval. Even after they came to know his real age, none of them seemed to object to the disparity in age between them. My father continued to enjoy their blessings, and they'd boast about how lucky my mother was to have the attention of such a distinguished gentleman. My father was a highly respected sergeant in the United States Army. He liked nice vehicles and made certain that he always kept one. He also enjoyed the nightlife and loved being out in the streets.

After a brief courtship, my parents were married on July 18, 1958. My sister was born in January of the following year, and I arrived two and a half years later. Shortly after I was born, my father was transferred to the Fort Knox Army Base in Kentucky, and soon afterward, my parents began having a lot of problems.

When my father retired from the army, my mother decided to put some distance between them since things weren't going well, and she discussed with him her plans to relocate to San Diego, California. My mother had an aunt who lived in San Diego and had heard many great things about the city. She believed that San Diego would be a great place to make a new start. Nevertheless, my father sought to keep their marriage together, so he decided to tag along with us to San Diego.

When we first arrived in San Diego, my parents went to work right away, trying to restore their marriage. In spite of this, things became volatile between them. My father's controlling demeanor triggered a lot of arguments — and many of them became physical. According to my mother, while she was eight months pregnant with my sister, my father stuck her as she tried to defend herself, and she nearly shoved him out of their second-story window. He initiated numerous fights with her in order to justify leaving home to run the streets, and my mother would find herself abandoned. My father sought to exert control over his young bride, but my mother wasn't going to let him control her without fighting back. She felt like she was living in hell.

My mother's role in her marriage was a stay-at-home mom, but she did her fair share of catering to my father, always making sure that the house was neat and tidy and that my father's favorite meals were prepared. Over the years, however, my parents' fighting proved

2

to be too much. Their marriage was on shaky ground, and a separation between them was imminent. My mother was forced to make the decision to either be a single parent or to remain in her dysfunctional marriage. After much contemplation, she asked my father for a separation, and my sister and I joined the swelling ranks of children growing up in fatherless homes. In the few years that I was exposed to my parents' marital dysfunction, I formed opinions about marriage. I would later emulate some of those behaviors in my own marriages.

I acquired some valuable life lessons from my relationships which transformed me into the person I am today. During some of my relationships, I had no peace. There was a lot of chaos, along with countless times I felt alone and isolated. I lived my life in fear of many things, and that fear left me immobilized. I feared making mistakes, feared truly enjoying my abundant life, and I even feared doing the things I loved most. I isolated myself from friends and family. My joy that once came from being around friends, laughing until it hurt and all of those other special things that made me happy, suddenly disappeared from my life. I relinquished to others the life that God had intended for me, as I became controlled by their weaknesses. I allowed my relationships to smother my inner-peace, and I became someone I didn't know. The people I had relationships with never asked me to surrender myself to them; it was of my own doing. I did it because I believed that it was required of me in order to have the successful relationships I craved. I became a people-pleaser who invested in everyone's life but my own — which eventually led to my own demise. I felt as if I was losing control.

God places different individuals in our lives. Some of them are placed in our lives for a season, while others remain in our hearts and minds for a lifetime. Each individual comes to leave an imprint on our hearts, and those imprints affect how we act, react, think, and

3

communicate with each other. It then becomes our assignment to identify how much time we allow each individual to stay and how much power we will relinquish to them to be able to influence our lives. We must make the choice! The decision is ours! It is essential that we accept the repercussions for our choices and take full accountability for them.

I was so engrossed in my addiction to dysfunction that I had become comfortable in my own misery and allowed other people's influences to immobilize my dreams. I surrendered a big part of myself to the men in my life. In turn, they used it against me as a means of control. During many years of self-reflection, I have discovered the effects that resulted from the amount of influence that I had relinquished to the five significant males who were part of my life. Each of these individuals deposited their own unique contributions; however, collectivity they have helped me write my life story. God has revealed the *life lessons* each one of them came to teach me. Some of the lessons I learned quickly, while the others nearly destroyed me.

My father came to teach *DISAPPOINTMENT.* It was my father who shaped my unrealistic expectations of marriage and family values. My father depicted a flawed picture of how a man should care for his wife and children. Those images set the stage for my future point of view. My father was absent during the majority of my life. His absence set me up for disappointment and unrealistic expectations that I would later impose on the males whom I would love.

My mother's boyfriend, John, came to teach the power of *CHOICES*. It was John who confirmed that no matter how financially stable a man is, if his character does not measure up to his generosity, then he simply isn't worth the trouble and a better choice must be made. Women frequently make the wrong choices when it comes to relationships with men. We habitually follow the examples shown to us. Unfortunately, the consequences of following such examples rob us of our joy and self-worth. We women must be strong enough to walk away from bad relationships, knowing that we are resilient enough to survive. We must learn to choose ourselves over the men who treat us badly. I thank God that my mother was able to walk away from the bad choice she made in John.

James came to teach *FORGIVENESS*. It was James who taught me that individuals can spend a lifetime seeking forgiveness from others for offenses they either unknowingly or knowingly caused. Forgiveness then becomes the catalyst for healing. James taught me the value of the words, "I'm sorry." It is very feasible for "I'm sorry" to be transformed into "You're forgiven" if individuals have the courage to ask for the forgiveness they seek. "I'm sorry," along with God's grace, can restore the brokenness in anyone.

Antoine came to teach *AWARENESS*. It was Antoine who taught me how important it is to be aware of who we allow into our lives. We often ignore the early-warning signs in our relationships. When ignored, those little red flags can generate a lot of heartache later. We must not be afraid to take the time to get to know the individuals with whom we seek to have intimate relationships. Having a keen awareness about our own brokenness can help increase our opportunity to enjoy a healthy, loving relationship. Two broken individuals simple cannot become united without addressing their past hurts. Both individuals must have the willingness to seek the assistance they need in order to be restored. The root cause of an individual's pain can be masked. Dysfunction then manifests itself into other areas of their lives. Antoine's brokenness came from childhood abandonment issues. I, too, experienced brokenness that resulted from the absence of my father. We failed to address our brokenness, and, as a result, our marriage suffered the consequences.

Deon came to teach *ACCEPTANCE.* It was Deon who taught me the power of accepting others for who they truly are. God holds us accountable for our actions. He can provide us with a loving partner who will challenge our ability to accept the good and bad in them. Those challenges are designed to help us develop patience and build trust. Patience is the key to accepting our partner for who they really are. True acceptance means that we must look beyond the other person's baggage and learn to accept them as the mate God intended them to be. Once that is accomplished, we are then challenged to learn to appreciate the positive attributes which each person brings to the relationship. Finally, we must all learn to accept our partners through true understanding. We should build each other up instead of tearing each other down.

It wasn't until I was nearly fifty years old that I realized God was with me through every aspect of my life. I was tired of living a life enslaved to dysfunction and feeling unworthy of being my once confident self. God showed me that He had prepared a perfect road map for me to live a successful life and that I am capable of having the life I desired. That successful life includes a healthy relationship with a loving partner — if I am willing to put in the work. God required me to let go of my past hurts and offences. I learned to trust God. I allowed Him to be in control, and He has healed my hurts and replaced them with self-love. I'm now living in God's purpose for my life. I am no longer addicted to dysfunction. He has released me to get out of the boat and to walk on the water. By walking on the water, I'm now empowered to seek the path of freedom. I'm free — *Released to live life out loud!*

CHAPTER 2

Disappointment: What a Father Brings

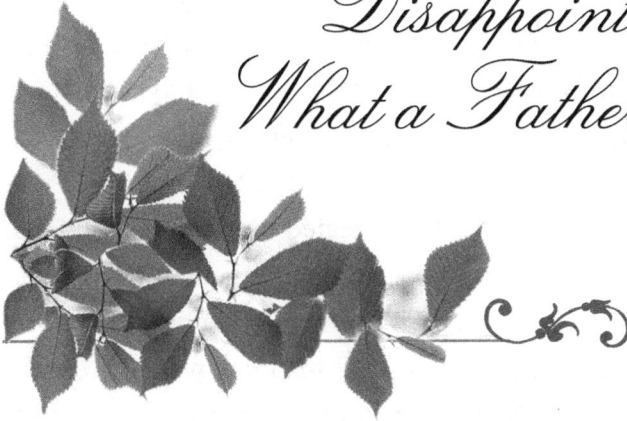

My mother had a formidable influence on my life, and, in fact, she is my role model. My mother is a strong, intelligent, and a respectable woman. Her mother died when she was two years old, so she was responsible for helping her father raise her two younger brothers. She did not have the benefit of having her mother's influence and guidance. As a result of my grandmother's absence, she and her two brothers were shuffled around between their paternal grandmother and their father while living a lackluster life. My grandfather rarely took an active parental role in their lives. Like many men, he saw his role as simply the financial provider. He had other priorities to concern himself with, one of which was his secret family who lived on the other side of town. My grandfather was a womanizer who fathered nine children. He was a handsome, brown-skinned man who stood about 5 feet 7 inches tall and weighed about 140 pounds. I'm not sure if he suffered from the "small man" syndrome. Nonetheless, he never had any problem getting the attention of the women he sought.

My mother witnessed many occurrences of physical abuse at the hands of her father to the many women he dated. There were also times when she became the victim of his anger. On some of those occasions, he inflicted both physical and verbal abuse on her. She internalized these accounts of abuse she received from him and decided early in her young life that she would not be a party to any physical abuse once she grew up. My grandfather's verbal abuse left her with deep emotional scars, too.

Some of the women he dated mistreated my mother and her brothers. She couldn't wait to grow up and release herself from under his thumb. My mother's experiences with caring for her brothers taught her how to be a good mother; her maternal instincts were developed by hands-on experience. She had the opportunity to utilize those skills once she gave birth to me and my sister.

My parents were faced with a lot of problems during their marriage. My mother realized that she had married a man who displayed similar qualities as her father. After several years of marriage, their union was doomed. When I was four years old, my parents relocated to San Diego, which was the beginning of what would become a permanent separation of many years for them. After many failed attempts to reconcile their marriage, my father made the decision to relocate to Brooklyn, New York. He'd done everything possible to keep his young family together, but it was too late.

Once my father relocated, he never returned to San Diego — not even once to visit us. We grew up without our father's presence. In turn, he never extended my sister and me an invitation to visit him. He became non-existent. I felt like a bastard child. My mother took on a dual parental role and did what she could to ensure that we had the basic necessities of life. She even worked two and sometime three jobs just to make ends meet. I'd ask my mother if she was all right after her long day. She'd reply, "Don't worry about me; I'm okay."

We moved around a lot. By the time I was in the fourth grade, I'd been to several different elementary schools. My sister and I learned how to take care of ourselves while our mother worked hard outside our home. We were very mature for our ages; we could dress ourselves and we walked a few miles to school every day. There were days when we were afraid that the big ferocious dog who lived on the corner would greet us. We were terrified when we saw him. I'd hold my sister's hand tightly as we would try to be elusive during our walk.

"Are you scared?" I'd ask her.

"Be real quiet and don't look nervous," she'd advise.

I'd felt as though I was going to pee my pants, but we always made it to school safely. We were happy when we finally moved out of that neighborhood. My mother never complained about the hand she was given in life; she never wasted her time being negative, nor did she dwell on how hard it was to be a single parent like many others who were in her shoes. My sister and I had a great childhood and our needs were always met. When my mother was a teenager, she was involved in a traumatic automobile accident, which caused her to be fearful of driving. We walked everywhere we needed to go — the grocery store, the laundromat, and other miscellaneous places. I enjoyed our walks; it was our time to bond, and we always had a good time. It always felt good to be outdoors, soaking up the sunshine, taking in the smells of the summer air, and being carefree children. We always stopped at the local ice cream parlor to get our favorite treat.

"I'm having mint chocolate chip — what about you guys?" my mother would be the first to announce.

"I'm having chocolate," my sister would reply.

"I'm having plain old vanilla," I'd chime in.

My sister and I were very close with my mother; I believe our closeness stemmed from the humble life we were forced to live. When I was in the fifth grade, my mother began dating a man who would later leave a great imprint on my life.

CHAPTER 3

Choices: A Boyfriend's Generosity

My mother met a man named John. She believed he was a great catch and they began to date exclusively. He was an ex-military cook who now worked on the base as a security guard. He was a hard-working man and a good provider. He gave us the good life by providing us with financial security, and he loved to go to various amusement parks.

"Where would you guys like to go this weekend?" he would ask.

"Knott's Berry Farm," I would always say. I loved going there, but it seemed like each time we went I got menstrual cramps.

When I was in the sixth grade, John moved my mother out of her small house into a brand-new one in a large newly-developed sub-division. I was very excited about the move; there were a lot of children to play with, and I started making new friends. John gave my mother all the material things a woman would expect from a man with a middle-class income. For the first time in my life I had my own room. I loved being in my own space. My sister and I shared a bathroom, and every now and then she would make a fuss about my leaving my things on her side of the sink. When my mother finally built up the courage to start driving again, John leased her several new vehicles within a short period of time.

"Surprise!" we'd hear him say each year.

"Thank you so much!" we'd hear her say, as she removed the big red bow from her Firebird.

My mother seemed happier than she had ever been, but she never wanted to marry John. He asked her several times, but she always said no.

CHAPTER 4

Disappointment: Daddy, I'm Disappointed

I t was 1973; I was in the sixth grade and enjoying my life completely. My mother told my sister and me that our father wanted to make a cameo appearance in our lives.

He confessed, "Ann, I want you and the girls to come to St. Louis."

"I'll have to get back with you," she replied.

My father wanted us to go there for a family visit, and my mother granted him permission to secure the airplane tickets. My father would drive his vehicle from Brooklyn to St. Louis. It was surprising that John agreed to let my mother go on the trip, since my father was going to be there.

The idea of seeing my father after so many years seemed awkward. It was never clear to me whether or not my parents had kept in touch with one another over the years. I was very excited to be going to St. Louis — I wanted to see the city where I was born. It seemed so mysterious to me, but most of my relatives lived there. I was finally going to get an opportunity to meet some of them, and I was ecstatic.

The first person I wanted to meet was my maternal grandfather —
I loved him even though this would be my first time meeting him. He
was the only living grandparent I had. My father picked us up from
the airport when we arrived. I sized him up and didn't see the family
resemblance.

"Look at my two angels. You've both gotten so big," he said as he
hugged us.

We smiled and anticipated what would happen next — he took my
sister and me to our grandfather's house. I believe my parents wanted
to spend some alone time together catching up. My grandfather was so
happy to see us. He provided me with some of my fondest memories
during our visit, like our trip to the local White Castle where he bought
my sister and me a couple of twenty-five cent hamburgers. It felt great
to take in the scenery of the inner-city streets. The people there seem
different from what I was used to.

"This hamburger sure is good," I bragged, as my grandfather
studied my silly expression.

"I'm glad you like it," he replied.

"We don't have White Castles in San Diego," I reported.

My grandfather was really sweet. I enjoyed spending time getting
to know him. When my parents came back for us, we went to meet
some of my father's family. First we visited a couple of his brothers'
houses and then his nieces' houses. He came from a big family which
consisted of several brothers and sisters. His family was very warm
and friendly to us. However, what seemed to interest me more that
meeting my father's family was being able to meet my mother's
brother. My mother has two brothers, but only one of them lives in
St. Louis, and that is my uncle Carl and his lovely wife Linda. They
welcomed us to stay at their house during our visit. My uncle Carl was
very nice, and I adored him.

"I can't believe how fast the girls have grown," my uncle said.

My mother replied, "Me neither," and they chuckled.

I was having a great time meeting everyone. Prior to going to St. Louis, the only family members who I had a relationship with were my mother and sister. Growing up without the benefit of having family around me caused feelings of loneliness for me, especially during holidays and birthdays. I felt abandoned by my relatives and often wondered what it would be like to have them around. I experienced a lot of disappointment from not being able to spend time with both my parents' extended families.

One of my best memories while visiting St. Louis was being able to meet my Uncle Carl's daughter Shree. I was six years older than she was, but I wasn't going to let our age difference get in the way of us having a great time together. I played every game she wanted to play, one of which was dolls, and we became instant best friends.

"Remember, I want you to bond with your dad," my mother reminded me.

It didn't seem to me that he was making an effort to get to know us. He didn't bring my sister and I any presents, and there were no shopping trips. He didn't do anything I expected a father to do while we visited with him. I was twelve years old and couldn't understand how he could be so inconsiderate. I felt so disrespected by him. I wanted to be spoiled by him and to feel loved, but there was a void. A few days into our visit, he told us that he would be leaving to return to Brooklyn. My father was ending early what was supposed to be our family vacation. The day he left, I was playing with my cousin, Shree, in her bedroom, and he entered her room to say goodbye.

My reaction to his leaving was subdued. I didn't really care that he was leaving and was certainly not surprised, since he had deserted us in the past. I wondered why he had planned the trip in the first place. I questioned his agenda. I believed he was attempting to get back together with my mother. Seeing my father brought me nothing but disappointment. It was at that very moment I realized his absence in my life really wasn't that earth-shattering, and his behavior during our visit gave me no reason to long for his presence in my life. We never formed a bond or emotional connection.

My father attempted to pick me up to kiss me on my forehead as part of his goodbye. I wondered if the man had lost his marbles. I wasn't the four-year-old little girl that he had left some years earlier. The way he attempted to lift me up made me feel violated. I wanted to ask him what he was doing, but I didn't. There was no reason for him to pick me up; it would have been perfectly acceptable for him to give me a hug or perhaps a handshake. He placed his hands securely under my rib cage and braced himself to lift me up. I felt like I was being lifted up by my breasts, which made me feel violated — and I didn't like it!

"Are you going to miss me?" he asked.

"Yes," I replied, but I was too afraid to be truthful with him.

My father disappeared from my life just as quickly as he had come, and I was left with new memories that were no different from the old ones. I didn't like him, but little did I know that it would be the last time I would see him alive. However, prior to his death, we did get the opportunity to talk. When I was almost eighteen years old, my father jumped through hoops to get my personal telephone number. I was still living at home with my mother when he made the random call to talk to me. When I picked up the receiver, I heard his voice on the other end.

"How are you doing, baby?" he asked, followed by, "I'm going to send you some money."

"Great," I replied.

I never asked my father for anything, so I thought it was pretty awesome that he wanted to send me some money. I was happy that he called and began to entertain the idea that we would develop a father-daughter relationship. A few weeks later, my father sent the money as promised, along with an unexpected envelope addressed to my mother. She looked inside the envelope and was surprised to find herself staring at some long-overdue divorce papers. My parents had been legally separated since I was four years old, and my father wanted to make things official. It seemed that his timing was centered on the fact that I was nearing eighteen years old. Once again, my father taught me disappointment. He used me as a go-between to deliver divorce papers to my mother. He didn't even consider how that would make me feel, but my mother didn't verbally express her anger toward my father's underhanded ploy.

"How do you feel about being served divorce papers after all these years?" I asked.

"Doesn't matter," she said.

My mother continued to rise above the drama. My next encounter with my father wouldn't be until some forty years later when I attended his funeral in Brooklyn. Even in his death, my father remained a stranger to me. Nonetheless, I forgave him and went on with my life.

CHAPTER 5

Choices: A Boyfriend from Hell!

Leaving St. Louis, we boarded our flight and headed back home to San Diego to our middle-class life with John. I developed a greater appreciation for him after visiting my father in St. Louis. I never called him Dad, but he was more of a father to me than my own.

Being back in San Diego was great. It was almost time for the new school year to start. My new school provided me with a lot of opportunities to make some special friendships. Those friendships would prove to be very important to me. The first day I walked into my new classroom, I was approached by a group of kids.

"Hey, do you know a girl named Robin? You guys look like twins," they informed me.

"No, I don't know her," I told them.

I soon had the opportunity to meet Robin; she was one of my classmates in my newly-assigned sixth-grade classroom. We hit it off immediately, and we both agreed with everyone else that we looked alike. We began to hang around each other all the time, and I started spending nights at her house. Her family liked me just as much as she did, and I felt like part of their family. We started telling people that we were cousins. Strangely enough, people who knew her believed that we were actually related. It felt good to be part of a two-parent family, since that was the one thing I longed for.

My mother and John began having a lot of problems, and my sister and I started to feel some tension between them. They argued behind the scenes, but I was never aware of their arguments until my sister brought it to my attention.

"Something real bad is going on between Mama and John," she reported.

"I never hear anything," I announced.

It seemed there was even some physical abuse going on behind the scenes. John was very jealous and controlling. My mother is a very attractive woman who stirred John's jealousy. She couldn't go anywhere or do anything without him. As a young girl, my mother made a promise to herself that she wouldn't be under any man's control, especially after being abused by her father and husband. A few years after we moved in with John, my mother told my sister and me that he was planning to visit his mother who lived out of town in Arkansas. She explained that we would be moving out while he was out of town. This meant leaving our middle-class life as we had come to know it. At the time, I didn't understand what was going on. I didn't realize that things between them were that bad. Everything felt so normal to me; however, my mother told me that she had to rethink her choices in life.

I tried to replay things about their relationship in my young mind. I wanted to recall anything that could have caused my mother to want to flee from John. I needed a better understanding of why my mother was acting this way, so I really thought hard about things. I was able to recall one instance. In fact, it stuck out as a red flag. The event was certainly problematic but provided me with some possible answers as to why my mother was in flight-fear mode. The event gave me some insight into her unhappiness with John. My mother had attempted to commit suicide and had nearly overdosed on some pills. She was trying to escape the pain that resulted from the turmoil she experienced while being with him. On the day in question, John explained to my sister and me that our mother was in the hospital.

"Is our mother going to be okay?" my sister asked him.

He was somewhat vague about the details and circumstances that had landed her there. John took us to San Diego's Navel Hospital to see her, and when we arrived, we learned that our mother needed to have her stomach pumped as a result of her alleged overdose of pills. The nurse reported that she was in stable condition and allowed us to see her. Our mother lay in her hospital bed, weak from the traumatic events of the day. I didn't know what to say to her. I was afraid and confused, and the incident left me with a lot of unanswered questions, yet we were all grateful to still have her with us. I often wondered what my mother was thinking. If she had succeeded in taking her own life, my sister and I would have been left with no one to care for us. At the time, I didn't realize that my mother's suicide attempt planted the seeds of suicide in my own young subconscious mind. I had no idea that I, too, would entertain the same suicidal thoughts. Just like my mother, suicidal thoughts were a means for coping with pain. My addiction to dysfunction fueled many of those thoughts.

So, when John went out of town to visit his mother, we moved out as planned. My mother moved us into a small two-bedroom apartment across town. For the first time in my young life, I was angry with her. I did not understand how she could throw away our middle-class lifestyle. I wondered how she could consider trading in our comfortable life for a substandard life in those low-income apartments. I was embarrassed to live there, and we certainly had a lot of adjustments to make. The biggest one for me was having to share a bedroom with my sister again, since she wasn't the easiest person to get along with. Another adjustment was getting used to seeing bugs. There were a lot of insects lingering around our apartment complex, which made me have to quickly conquer my fear of water bugs. When the darkness of the night fell, it seemed like thousands of them surrounded the inoperable swimming pool in the middle of our apartment complex. It was a really disgusting sight. I also had to give up some of my freedom, and I no longer had the ability to choose how long I wanted to play outside. The landlord of the apartment complex was a short, middle-aged man who loved to enforce the apartment's curfew. When the apartment complex's lights came on in the evening, it was time to go inside. If you were one of the unlucky children caught playing outside after curfew, your parents were charged a fine.

It became apparent that my mother had made the right choice to leave John. A week after we moved out of the brand-new house that he had purchased for her, he returned home to find it empty and became enraged and wanted revenge. John then went on a mission to locate us and turned into an enraged lunatic with a gun. One afternoon, while I was sitting outside on a friend's porch who lived in our apartment complex, I noticed a man in a car who had a strong resemblance to *"my father figure"*, John, looking at me and waving a loaded gun in my direction.

"Run!" my friend screamed.

We were all scared to death and scrambled for safety. I ran as fast as I could to our apartment to warn my mother that he had found us. In his anger, he became larger than life. He stood about 6'2", weighed about 245 lbs, and had a stocky build and an intimidating demeanor. Since he didn't see where I had run, he began interrogating the neighborhood children, "Where does Benita live?" he demanded.

He was determined to get information from them. He was successful, and the information he received led him straight to our front door. I ran into our apartment, locked the door, and called out for my mother. My heart was beating so fast as I warned her that he was coming. She realized that her safety and possibly ours was in jeopardy. I truly believe that she was afraid of him. If he had found his way into our apartment, he was capable of inflicting bodily harm to her.

John started pounding on our door and yelling, "Ann, open up the goddamn door!" he commanded.

We could hear the anger in his voice. He pounded on the door for what seemed like an eternity, but it was actually only about a half an hour. My mother decided not to call the police, and we waited nervously until he left our apartment complex. That night, we breathed a sigh of relief that things hadn't become worse than they had. That was the last time I would ever see John. My mother ended her relationship with him, and we continued to live in those apartments.

The stress from their breakup and the move really took a toll on her. I noticed that within a few months she lost a significant amount of weight. She was looking good, and she had moved on with her life. As we settled into our new life, I realized that she had made some positive choices. It took a lot of courage for her to leave John, and I was proud of her for having the courage to leave. My mother provided my sister and me with a positive example of a strong woman by demonstrating that women shouldn't stay in toxic environments.

CHAPTER 6

A Teenager's Transformation

It was 1975; I began to transform into a mature teenager. As I began to re-adjust to living in our apartment complex, I started to like living there. I formed some great friendships. However, I began to miss Robin and all the friends I had made from my old neighborhood. We had been very close. Moving meant that I wouldn't be able to see them as often as I once did. I found out through a mutual friend that Robin and her family were moving from San Diego to Lemon Grove, California. Her parents didn't want her to go through the transition of moving and starting a new school alone. They were aware of my mother's situation with John and our recent move, and they believed that they had a reasonable solution to both our dilemmas and paid my mother a visit to discuss the possibility of my living with them for a while. After a lengthy discussion, my mother agreed to allow me to move in with them temporarily. I suspect that she felt guilty for uprooting me from my friends and our middle-class lifestyle. My mother and my sister kept each other company while I went to live with Robin.

Robin and I were starting the eighth grade at our new school. Our new junior high school was very small. In fact, there were only a few Black students who attended. The teachers and students loved us, and they also thought we were twins. They complimented us by telling us how pretty we were, and we became popular very quickly.

Robin began dating an Asian boy named Ted who attended our school. I was attracted to an Italian boy name Jimmy and really had a crush on him. He was very cute. He had some distinctive Italian features, like thick eyebrows and curly black hair. He was one of the first boys to reject me, but he encouraged my flirting even though he didn't share the same attraction for me. After about two months, he began to pursue an Italian girl named Laura who lived in our neighborhood, and I was crushed!

"I like you as a friend," he told me, and I had to get over him pretty quickly.

It was really fun living with Robin, and I felt comfortable in their home. She had a sister and a brother, and her parents were also the caretaker of their nephew. We loved to play cards and listen to Richard Prior comedy albums. For hours we would recite his comedic material verbatim and laugh until it hurt. We loved being around one another. Living at their house provided me with yet another opportunity to enjoy a middle-class lifestyle. Their neighborhood was very similar to the one I had become accustomed to while living with John. They had an outdoor pool and loved to participate in outdoor activities. I loved her family's dynamics and often wished I had been born into their family. I wanted them to accept me so that I could stay with them long-term. I didn't want to give anyone else the opportunity to uproot me from my middle-class lifestyle again. I liked being part of their stable family, and it was nice to see both her parents living under the same roof and working toward the same goals. Robin's parents both had careers and worked fulltime, and they seemed to have the perfect marriage.

After we settled in their new home, Robin and I went from house to house, attempting to secure babysitting jobs. The White families in their neighborhood were very receptive to the idea of having two thirteen-year-old Black teenage girls babysit for them. There was one family in particular who hired me to babysit their children often. They entrusted me with the care of their eight-month-old daughter and their sons who were three and five, and they loved for me to babysit for them. I would read to the children, play games with them, and always have them tucked securely in their beds prior to their parents' return. I was the family's first choice whenever they needed a babysitter.

I lived with Robin and her family for about a year, but just prior to my completing the ninth grade, her parents informed my mother that it was time for me to return home. They didn't provide any specific reasons for their abrupt request for me to leave, but they hinted around about some financial concerns they faced. I resented them for a long time for sending me back home to my sub-standard lifestyle, because I didn't believe they were being sincere with my mother. Nonetheless, I returned home only to be reminded that I shared a cramped room with my sister. She didn't seem to embrace my return. She was nearly a senior in high school and had enjoyed her privacy in my absence.

My mother enrolled me in Gompers Junior High, a predominately Black junior high school. It certainly was going to be a big change for me since I was accustomed to attending predominately White and multi-cultural schools. I was convinced that making the transition from those types of environments to an all Black one was going to be very intimidating for me.

Prior to starting school, I began hanging around with all my good friends again. Most of them were boys who had a crush on me. I had a lot of choices, as they all competed for my attention. I really didn't take any of them seriously, but it was the first time in my life that I received so much attention, and I liked it.

I never really thought of myself as being attractive. In fact, I had a complex when I was growing up. I had very skinny stick legs and a big butt my sister and my cousins teased me about a lot. They said my butt looked like it was sitting on my back, which caused me to develop a complex. I kept my butt covered with a coat or jacket and always made sure I alternated between the two even on the hottest days. Once the boys in my apartment complex started pursuing me, I didn't know how to respond to them. I was interested in a Samoan boy name Jerry who lived down the street from my apartment complex. The fact that I liked him really caused a lot of problems for me, because the Black boys who lived in my apartment complex took offense to me liking him because he wasn't Black. They began pressuring me to break up with him, and I finally caved in.

"Jerry, I don't like you anymore. It's over," I told him.

I broke up with Jerry for no apparent reason and really hurt his feelings. I pretended to like one of the Black boys who lived in my apartment complex just to appease them. I had some good female friends I liked to hang around with too. It was nice hanging out with them, although they were a few years younger than me. We would run all over our apartment complex while acting young and carefree.

I completed my ninth-grade year at Gompers Junior High. There were a few fights, but for the most part I survived. It wasn't as bad as I had imagined it would be. The summer prior to starting the tenth grade, I began to babysit again. I accepted a job to babysit for a young single mother who lived in my apartment complex. She had a four-year-old daughter named Tina and a set of twin boys she called Big Man and Little Man. I babysat nearly ten hours a day for her and took great care of her children. I was only fourteen years old and working a full-time job, but my mother didn't approve of me spending all my time babysitting.

"You need to be enjoying your life. You're too young to be tied up with those kids all day," she would remind me.

My mother was right, especially since I wasn't making a lot of money for all the long hours I worked. I started to feel like I was the mother of those children. I enjoyed caring for them, but it was time for me to start having some fun of my own again. I had a passion for children and loved to babysit; nonetheless, I quit my job shortly before the school year began.

CHAPTER 7

Those Awesome High School Years

It was 1977; I was starting high school. My mother enrolled me in one of the most notorious Black high schools in San Diego, but she didn't have any other options since we lived in that school district. Lincoln High School had a bad reputation, and I honestly didn't know how I was going to survive. Their reputation was far worse than Gompers Junior High. My sophomore year at LHS went without incident. I made a few friends, joined a few clubs, and minded my own business. I started getting a lot of attention from the senior boys. One of them was the older brother of Marcus Allen who later went on to play football for the Oakland Raiders.

The senior boys were on a quest to see how many young girls they could lure into having sex with them. They wanted bragging rights for the amount of notches they were able to add to their belts. I wasn't going to have sex with any of them. I was a good girl! I must admit that I liked making out with a couple of them occasionally, but I wanted to refrain from having sex for as long as I could. The senior boys quickly lost interest in me, and the feeling was mutual.

31

My junior year at LHS proved to be the start of my becoming comfortable in my own skin. The summer prior to starting my junior year, I often went to my high school to watch the Youth Pee Wee Football and cheerleading team practices. One day while I was observing them, I was approached by an old friend, Dee. She was there practicing for the upcoming high school cheerleading tryouts.

"Benita, do you like cheerleading? Come join our practice," she said.

One of my deepest desires was to be a high school cheerleader. I had previously tried out for the cheerleading squad while living with Robin at my old school, but I didn't make the squad. I quickly removed my coat that covered my butt and joined their practice. It was at that moment I realized that I was a really good cheerleader. My peers were trying out for spots on the senior varsity squad. It didn't bother me that I was trying out for a spot on the junior varsity squad. I was content that I tried out and made it. Everyone on the squad was delighted to have me as their team member, and they voted for me as their team captain. It was an honor and privilege to be a cheerleader at LHS. We had a rich history of tradition that included some of the best homecoming celebrations. Dee and I became best friends and were inseparable. She had a lot of style and she dressed well, and some of her style rubbed off on me while some of my charisma rubbed off on her. We were very popular. She was voted best dressed and I was voted best smile, and our names will live on forever as part of the rich history at LHS.

It was 1979; I became a senior, and cheerleading was still a big part of my life. I competed for a spot on the varsity squad and made the team. In my opinion, I was one of the best on our squad. My friend Lisa and I would collaborate to make a lot of the motions for our new cheers. Many of the cheers at LHS were traditional ones that

32

were passed down from generation to generation. Part of the tradition included cheerleaders from previous years returning to cheer at the homecoming game. Homecoming celebrations were heavily attended by alumni, and it was exciting be part of the festivities. I had some of the best times of my life while attending LHS.

I became involved in an academic college preparation program called Upward Bound while still in high school. The program had a profound influence on my life and provided me with a sense of family. I developed a strong desire to attend college, and the UB program staff really cared about everyone's success. They motivated all the students who attended the program to pursue a post-secondary education. During our senior year, Dee and I enjoyed all that high school had to offer. We loved all our friends and they made us laugh often. The only thing missing for me was a steady mature boyfriend. I wasn't attracted to any of the boys at my high school, as they all seemed so immature. I concluded that if I was going to find a steady boyfriend, he certainly didn't attend LHS, and I realized that I was going to have to look elsewhere.

CHAPTER 8

Forgiveness: A First Love's Impact

During the last basketball game of the season of my senior year, our team was scheduled to play a rival school. While at the game, I met a young man who would have a significant impact on my life. The basketball game was being played on their court, and I was engaged in the game as we cheered our team on. It was a very close game, and there was a lot of electricity in the air. He was a tall, handsome young man with a large afro, but initially I wasn't interested in him, although he did seem charming.

"My name is James. What's your telephone number?" he asked.

James was a recent graduate. I wanted to get to know him, so I gave him my number. The game was heavily attended by a lot of alumni who wanted to be included in the bragging rights if their team won. To my surprise, we lost the game that evening.

A few days later, James called me and we seemed to hit it off right away. We began seeing each other often, and I took a real liking to him. He visited me at my mother's apartment, even though we lived on opposite ends of town. He and his family lived comfortably in the same middle-class neighbor where we had once lived with John. I still lived in the less than desirable area with my mother. We spent a lot of time making out on her couch. He was well-mannered, and it seemed like months before he ever attempted to be intimate with me. I began to wonder why he had not asked me to go all the way. I was perplexed. After all, most of the other boys my age always had one thing in mind — and that was having sex.

I finally built up the nerve to ask him, "James, why haven't you asked to go all the way with me?"

He just chuckled. James was a real gentleman and wasn't in a rush like most of the boys I knew. We had been dating for nearly six months, so after we had that conversation, it goes without saying that we became intimate right away. I began to fall in love with James, and my heart seemed to skip a beat whenever he came around. My senior prom was approaching quickly, and I wanted him to attend it with me. I wanted to have an opportunity to show him off to all my classmates. I wanted them to know that I had a boyfriend who was an outsider. It was my quest to be the envy of all the girls at LHS. He was certainly a good catch.

"James, my prom is coming up. Will you take me?" I asked.

"I can't. I don't have the money. I just attended my own prom last year," he conveyed.

I was devastated to learn that he couldn't go with me. I didn't find fault with him for not being able to go, since the excuse he provided made perfect sense to me. I had to come up with a plan "B", so I asked a good friend who attended the same rival school as James to escort me. James didn't have a problem with me attending my prom with someone other than him, so my friend agreed to accompany me with "no strings attached". At the time, I really didn't think much of James' rejection, although it did hurt my feelings. He made it up to me by attending my senior grad night, and I was very excited to take him. Grad night is a yearly event that is held at Disneyland in Anaheim, California for graduating seniors from all over California. We had a good time, and I was relieved that I didn't have to be with anybody other than him that night.

CHAPTER 9

Forgiveness: Just Ask For It

After graduating high school, I completed my requirements for the UB program on the campus of San Diego State University. I planned to attend SDSU in the fall as an incoming freshman. That summer, I had no idea that my world would be turned upside down. One afternoon while I was talking to a friend in my dorm room, she revealed that she had attended a concert at a local venue over the weekend. I took in all the details about the concert. It seemed to be fun.

"We had a really good time. This guy named Lamont and his brother James went with us," she bragged.

I continued to listen carefully; I could tell by her description that it was the same James who belonged to me. She went on to explain that Lamont and James brought dates. I was shaken and devastated by the information. I couldn't believe that "my James" was a two-timer. While I was spending weekends studying at the UB program, he was busy courting another young lady. I wondered why he had deceived me and felt so betrayed that I couldn't wait to confront him about the situation.

I telephoned James immediately, and I confronted him when I reached him, "Where were you on Saturday night?" I demanded.

He was caught him off guard and quickly denied the allegations, but I was relentless as I continued to badger him for answers.

"I was at the concert with Hazel, who is a friend, my brother, and his girlfriend," he declared. "Who told you?" he wanted to know.

"It's not relevant," I replied.

I realized that I knew his date; I had met Hazel some years earlier when she visited her cousins who lived in my apartment complex. It was apparent that she was more than just a friend to him.

"I'm not going to be part of your love triangle," I told James.

It wasn't my style, so I broke off my relationship with him. Both Hazel and I were causalities of love and of James' deception. Neither of us had known that we were competing for his attention.

It was the fall of 1979; I began my first semester of college at SDSU. My best friend Dee and I were freshmen. We were having the time of our lives on campus and decided to live at home to save money. Dee and I went to a lot of parties, enjoyed all the good food on campus, and even considered trying out for a spot on the SDSU cheerleading squad. It was a magical time and also the same year Michael Jackson's hit single "Off the Wall" came out. I was finally getting over James, and my broken heart was beginning to mend.

James and Hazel also attended SDSU, and we shared a few awkward moments on campus. Each time I ran into them, my heart shattered as they walked the campus holding hands. I attempted to change my route to avoid seeing them. After a few months, James and Hazel broke up because she wanted out of the relationship. It wasn't long before he came back to me to reconcile our relationship, and of course I took him back because I had never stopped loving him.

40

It was 1980; James and I were dating exclusively, and I was so happy that we were finally a legitimate couple. Things were going pretty good for us, and we were spending a lot of time going on dates instead of only hanging out at my mother's apartment. We hung out with his brother and his girlfriend at their apartment. He started introducing me to more members of his family. However, as time passed, I began to feel less confident about our relationship; it felt like something was missing, but I couldn't put my finger on what was wrong. I was clearly more engaged in our relationship than he was. I realized that he really liked me a lot, but I wanted more from him. His mother taught me an early life-lesson when she found out I had purchased for him a Member's Only jacket.

"Don't buy James things. You never have to pay for a man's attention," she advised me.

I appreciated her candor. I was unable to handle all the mixed feelings and emotions I had for him and decided to break up, although I really didn't have a good reason to. When I delivered the news, he didn't seem to have any objections to my request.

James and I went our separate ways — so we thought. Our breakup didn't seem to make me any happier; I was miserable. I began to sink into a dark place. I was depressed but didn't realize it. I'd never felt that way before about anyone. He was my first love, and I wanted him feel what I was feeling. I wanted him to love me, too. After all, the other male figures in my life prior to him had already disappointed me. I wanted James to be the right choice for me. I needed more than just my immediate family to love me. I believed that James was the person who would.

I was feeling suicidal after I broke off my relationship with him. I started entertaining thoughts of suicide and ways to end my young life. While I was driving home one evening from my cousin's house,

I envisioned myself using a razor blade to slit my wrist while driving down a hilly road into oncoming traffic. I stopped at a convenience store for the razor blades that I planned to use. A part of me really wanted to end my life, while the other part just wanted to get James' attention. I needed to know that he really cared about me. I wanted him to validate his feelings for me right then and there and to reassure me that my love for him wasn't based on deception. I decided to give James one last opportunity to confess his feelings for me, so I called him and began to sob profusely as he answered the telephone.

"James, I'm calling to say goodbye," I told him.

I told him about my suicide plan. He seemed taken aback and showed immediate concern. He frantically began to talk me out of my plans. Once I felt a little better, he reprimanded me for my disturbing behavior.

"You go straight home and call me," he demanded.

"I will," I mumbled.

That conversation saved my life that evening! I was convinced that he really did care about me. Our breakup had affected me more than I could have ever imagined.

CHAPTER 10

Forgiveness: My Deepest Regret

We didn't get back together, but we couldn't seem to let each other go. The more I attempted to pull away from him, the more he sought after me. Our going back and forth made it difficult for me to move on. We were too young and immature to deal with the strong feelings we had for each other. We continued to be intimate and spent many hours talking on the telephone. A few months after my suicidal episode, I noticed that I had missed my period. I went to the clinic to take a pregnancy test and found out that I was pregnant. I was carrying James' baby. I was nineteen years old, but the news of having a baby made me happy. James came from a good family, was a college student, a great person, and had a bright future ahead of him. He certainly had all the attributes I wanted for the father of my unborn child. I thought he would make an excellent father. There were many occasions when I observed him interacting with his nephew; he was very loving and playful. I really didn't know how he was going to take the news of my pregnancy. I also had some apprehension about having our baby because I was taking birth control pills and feared that I may have consumed some during the time of my conception. I didn't want to give birth to a stillborn or deformed baby.

The first person who I told I was pregnant was my best friend Dee. I knew I could trust her.

"Dee, I'm so excited! I'm going to be a mom!" I proclaimed.

She was a little pessimistic and wondered if I was ready to take on such a big responsibility.

"Are you sure you're ready?" she asked.

"As ready as I will ever be," I replied.

I wondered if I should tell my mother the news, because I realized that she would be disappointed, and I didn't want to break her heart. I decided to keep the news of my pregnancy from her. She had warned us about the possibility of my getting pregnant when she caught us having sex in my bedroom one evening after she returned home. As my mother opened the front door of our apartment, she caught a glimpse of James' naked backside as he ran from my bedroom into the bathroom across the hall.

She really gave us a stern talk, "If you're going to be screwing around, it won't be under my roof! Are we clear?" she announced.

We heard her loud and clear. It was certainly a conversation that neither of us would forget. My mother was always so proud of my accomplishments that breaking the news to her about my pregnancy was a big deal. I was never concerned about how I would provide for my baby financially. I was blessed to have a good union job with excellent medical benefits. I was also an experienced caretaker, which was a skill I had developed in my youth. I could have easily become a single parent if that was my choice. I was perplexed. I had to tell James that I was pregnant, but I really wasn't sure how he would react. I wanted him to be just as thrilled as I was. I imagined a bright future with him and our child. He was the youngest of six children — the pride and joy of his parents. They would be crushed if they found out that he had a baby on the way.

I was very nervous the night I delivered the news to him, "James, I'm pregnant," I reported.

His initial reaction was anger. I watched him jump out of my vehicle to pace the sidewalk. He looked like he had just received the worst news of his life. His reaction made me feel very sad inside, and I realized that I had just delivered devastating news that he simply wasn't equipped to handle. James was overwhelmed and had no idea how he was going to tell his parents, nor did he have the courage to break their hearts. He was in a tight spot, since he'd grown up as a Catholic, and they believed that having an abortion was not an option. All of those dynamics caused James a lot of stress.

"Can we take a day or so to allow ourselves some time to consider our options?" he asked.

Once James had the opportunity to digest all the information given to him, he calmed down and we discussed our dilemma over the telephone. He didn't seem to have any answers or suggestions about how we should handle our dilemma. I wished for a particular outcome. I wanted him to tell me that everything would be okay, but he didn't. He just sat there in silence on the other end of the telephone. After spending a considerable amount of time going over the facts, I made the decision for both of us.

"I'm going to begin making telephone calls to inquire about the cost of an abortion," I told him.

I really wanted to have our baby, but I wasn't going to force him into becoming a father, especially when he wasn't ready. As a child, I had always dreamed about being a mother someday and wanted the person who fathered my child to be ecstatic once they learned the news of my pregnancy. Having a baby with someone who didn't feel

45

the same enthusiasm as I did didn't seem to resonate with me. As much as I loved him and his baby that was growing inside of me, I decided to let him off the hook. He, too, agreed that it was the best thing to do. I based my decision to have an abortion on James' unique situation. He was relieved and assured me that he would be by my side throughout the entire process.

It was January 1981; I made the appointment to terminate my first baby by the man I loved. It was certainly the hardest thing I ever had to do. I never imagined how devastating our decision to abort our baby would be, not only for me but for James also in the long term.

When we arrived at the facility, I checked in with the receptionist at the front desk. She pointed me in the direction of the waiting room, and as I waited for my named to be called, I started to feel sick to my stomach. I was so scared and nervous.

Soon, I heard the sound of my name being called, "Benita, please follow me to the examination room," the nurse said.

I was instructed to get completely undressed. I followed the instructions and nervously waited for the doctor to come into the room to provide me with the details about the procedure.

"You will be placed under anesthesia for about an hour," the doctor briefly explained, and I acknowledge that I understood.

After the procedure was over and my anesthesia wore off, I woke up and found myself in the recovery room. I began to panic and became hysterical. I started screaming as tears rolled down my face. I was devastated. The attending nurse quickly came over and attempted to calm me down. She had a cold demeanor.

"Miss, you're going to have to be quiet. Other women are here for the same reason as you," she demanded.

That was her way of letting me know that others had come to terminate their babies.

"Your screams are upsetting them," she blurted out.

I wasn't concerned about anyone else's feelings but my own. All I could think about was the fact that I had just aborted my child by the man I loved. There wasn't anything anyone could say or do to make me feel any better or any worse about the situation. It was apparent that even she wasn't going to attempt to show me any compassion.

An overwhelming sense of sadness engulfed my being, and I began to feel depressed right away. I resented James and didn't want to have anything to do with him. He would certainly feel the wrath of my anger. I questioned myself about our actions, and I wanted to hold him responsible for not asking me to keep our baby. When I returned back to the waiting area where I had left James sitting some hours earlier, he also was visibly crushed. The reality of our decision to abort our baby had taken a toll on both of us.

"Are you okay?" he asked. "I resisted the urge to rescue you while you were going through with the horrific procedure," he told me.

His declaration of guilt caused me to despise him ever more. It was too late; the damage was already done, and there was nothing we could do about it. The car ride back to my house seemed like it took hours as we rode in silence. I couldn't wait to get home and as far away from him as I could. In the days that followed, I didn't want to talk to him and made every attempt to avoid seeing him. My goal was to put the episode behind me as quickly as possible. Seeing or talking to him would only prolong my healing. I wanted to get on with my life, but I realized that he would always be a constant reminder of our decision to abort our baby. I wanted to escape that reality. I immersed myself in work and secured a second job in a fast-food restaurant as an assistant manager. Between my two jobs, I worked a lot of hours. I was determined to move on with my life. It wasn't very long before James found out where my second job was, and he began to make frequent visits there. I resented his presence. He was violating my private space, and I was still very upset with him.

"Benita, we need to talk," he told me.

I believed that if I avoided him long enough I would be able to forget about the recent events, but he was determined and relentless in his attempts to seek forgiveness. After a few months passed, my anger began to dissipate and I was ready to talk to him again. We began talking a lot on the telephone, and our relationship slowly began to transform into a loving friendship. Although it was difficult for me to get over him, I was determined to make every attempt to do so.

My best friend Dee and I started going out a lot to dance, and we were always in the company of good friends. Some of them were gay male friends who loved to hang out, and we always had a blast with them. Dee was a better dancer than me, but we both made excellent dance partners for the individuals who lined up to dance with us. We were often the winners of a few local dance contests, and we always had a really good time. A co-worker of ours from the San Diego Zoo told us about a great place to go dancing that was on the naval base. Initially we considered the idea to be laughable, given the fact that we were allergic to sailors. We spent many of our lunch breaks laughing at all the newly active sailors who made the San Diego Zoo a mandatory destination. They dressed in those silly-looking crackerjack uniforms and always seemed awkward in their mannerisms. We made a promise never to date a sailor, and we thought most of them were unattractive. Nevertheless, we decided to be adventurous and paid the Navy Club a visit one Friday night. We were pleasantly surprised to find that the atmosphere was rather lively. There were plenty of single sailors to dance the night away with, and surprisingly they were all dressed in civilian clothing, which made them look more attractive. One thing I found beneficial about going to the Navy Club was that it served as an outlet in helping me to get over James.

It didn't take long for us to become frequent visitors. Loving all the attention we received whenever we walked through the door, we enjoyed getting all dressed up in our best outfits for each appearance, and we knew we looked gorgeous. It was easy for us to make a lot of friends with the regulars who thought we carried ourselves in a respectful way, which was different than some of the other women who frequented the Navy Club. Dee and I just wanted to have a good time dancing, but a few of the sailors were seeking more than just dance partners.

James and I were becoming distant. Our conversations transitioned to us sharing stories about the different directions our lives were taking. It no longer seemed to bother me that he was dating other people. I allowed him to talk freely about the direction his life was taking and the people in it, and I began to consider seeing other people as well. The more I went to the Navy Club, the more I noticed potential suitors and changed my mind about dating them. Dee changed her mind too and began seriously dating a sailor. I was waiting for the right one to come along. I was attracted to a couple of them but still had some reservations. I placed them on my "short list" of potential suitors. I met them on different occasion. They seemed nice, were great dancers, and I enjoyed their conversations. I made a mental note that when we returned to the Navy Club, the first one of them that I came in contact with would be the one to benefit from all my time and attention.

CHAPTER 11

Awareness: Warning, Marriage Can be Hard

When Dee and I returned to the Navy Club, I surveyed the room to see if any of those men on my short list were there. To my surprise, I saw one of them and recalled that his named was Antoine.

"Do you think we could get to know each other better?" he inquired.

I didn't hesitate to give him my telephone number, and we danced the entire night away.

When it was time for the Navy Club to close, he asked Dee for a ride back to his barracks located on the naval base. Antoine's request seemed awkward since we had driven there in Dee's two-seated sports car. She agreed to give him a ride, despite the lack of room. He sat on my lap during the short ride, which gave me an extra opportunity to check him out.

The events of that night were significant, and I had no idea that he would become my future husband. He was a clean-cut young man from Newark, New Jersey, who stood about 5'10", with a small build, and he was very interesting. We began seeing each other daily in the apartment I shared with Dee. We loved to walk over to the local 7-11 to play their Miss Pac Man arcade game, and we would compete with each other to see who could get the highest score. Sometimes we played the arcade games for hours. He beat me often, and we always completed our evenings devouring vanilla Hagen Dazs ice cream and relaxing.

Antoine and I spent a lot of time together going on inexpensive dates. We frequented all the San Diego tourist attractions, such as: The San Diego Zoo, Sea World, Wild Animal Park, the beaches, and the local parks. He had a unique style that I wasn't used to, but I liked the way he carried himself. I certainly wanted to spend more time getting to know him since he was very charming. Unlike the other men in my life, he seemed more than willing to give me all the attention I deserved. By having him in my life, my feelings for James began to dissipate. Antoine and I became serious pretty quick. I also liked his sense of humor and his willingness to be adventurous.

By my lack of enthusiasm when he called to talk, James began to sense that he had some competition. He attempted to regain my attention by occasionally showing up at my job without notice, but it became apparent that he had allowed someone else to take me away from him. He was right; I was falling in love with Antoine.

We dated for about eight months and got married shortly thereafter. I was still so naïve regarding relationships that I ignored a few red flags early on. I wanted so badly to be married that I pressured Antoine into marrying me when he was only nineteen and I was twenty-one. We were certainly too young, and I didn't even afford him the opportunity to propose to me. I had decided that we were getting married, and I wasn't taking no for an answer.

One night while we were sitting at home watching television, I convinced him to marry me. I then called a justice of the peace, "Can you come over right away and marry us?" I asked.

"I only take cash, but I am willing to come right over," he advised me.

Antoine was surprised by my forwardness but agreed to go along with my suggestion. Our marriage was such an impromptu event that the only people who attended were the three of us. I dressed myself in a black taffeta short dress that I had previously worn to another social event, while he wore a dark-blue suit to my liking. I was in such a rush to get married that I didn't even invite my own mother. That night I became Antoine's wife, to the surprise of our friends and family, and I finally got my wish.

Antoine was a good husband, and at first he was very sweet and kind to me. We seemed to understand each other's personalities and quirkiness, but as time went on, I began to learn a lot more about him that really surprised me. It seemed that I really didn't know him at all. He wanted me to believe that he was someone different than he actually was, because he was embarrassed about his actual life. He lied when he introduced me to his alter ego and fictitious fantasy family: A two-parent working-class family who resided in a brownstone building in Brooklyn, New York. They were successful and had a lot of money. Of course, I was attracted to what seemed to be a great life, especially since my father also lived in Brooklyn, but Antoine later recanted his story. I then learned that he was actually a victim of abandonment. He came from a broken family that had some undesirable family dynamics. I also noticed things about his personality that I wasn't aware of. He was a little hotheaded and had a short fuse, especially when provoked. One day, I was looking through some of his personal belongings. I found a precious picture of a baby boy in his Holy Quran. I was looking through his Holy Quran because he was an occasional practicing Muslim and I wanted to learn more about his religion and its practices.

"Whose beautiful baby is that?" I questioned.

"Why did you go through my stuff?" he asked.

"You're avoiding the question about the baby," I said.

At that point, I realized that he had not been truthful with me. He had a child that he had not told me about. "The baby is mine," he announced after a few minutes had passed.

"Well, he sure is cute," I told him.

His child had been born out of wedlock with a childhood girlfriend who lived in Newark, New Jersey. I thought their baby boy was adorable. Once I digested the fact that he had a child, I began to entertain the ideal of having a child of my own. However, this time there would be no excuses not to have my child. I was married and believed that there was nothing wrong with wanting to start a family. Antoine believed that we needed to wait awhile. He wanted us to enjoy each other, so I agreed to wait.

As time passed, I began to see that my preconceived notions about marriage were drastically different from what I was actually experiencing. We were so young that neither of us knew anything about being a good spouse to the other. Like me, Antoine was also a statistic that had grown up in a fatherless home, but not only had he grown up fatherless, he'd also grown up motherless. He had been abandoned as a baby by his parents for his paternal grandparents to take care of until their death some years later. Our marriage was plagued with problems from the onset, and the problems we faced seemed to get bigger over time. When we got married, I kept my job at the San Diego Zoo. I worked there as a Food Service Leader for a few years. Antoine continued on in the United States Navy.

About a year after our wedding, he was released with a service discharge resulting from violations of military policies, and it wasn't long before Antoine starting indulging in drugs. Initially I didn't see his drug use as a problem. I didn't smoke marijuana so I wasn't going to judge him for smoking it.

The biggest issue that we faced in our marriage was derived from my perspective of the perfect marriage. I expected to have a perfect marriage with a perfect husband without brokenness. I had no awareness that there was no such thing! When Antoine couldn't deliver on that promise, I became miserable. My perspective of the perfect marriage came from the images I saw on television programs like *Leave It to Beaver* and *The Brady Bunch*. Those programs depicted men who were perfect husbands with perfect families. I found Antoine's imperfections to be a contradiction to the ideal husband I expected him to be, so I became disappointed. I certainly didn't want my marriage to mirror any of the dysfunctional examples that my parent's had demonstrated. It seemed as if Antoine's main priority was to hang out with his navy friends and smoke marijuana daily, and his desire to get high intensified over the years. I began to feel increasingly disappointed by his choices.

My unhappiness transitioned into a state of depression. My demons were returning to haunt me, and I began to entertain suicidal thoughts, just as I had in my prior relationship with James. My awareness for the root cause of my depression eluded me. The more depressed I became, the more erratic my behavior. Antoine purchased a small handgun for our protection. One evening, while we were engaged in an intense argument, I took the handgun from its stored location and ran into an alley adjacent to our condo. I intended to use the handgun to shoot myself.

"Stop! Let me talk to you!" he yelled as he ran after me.

Antoine chased me up the alley, attempting to stop me, but I ran as fast as I could to get away from him. I believed that by killing myself I would ease the pain I felt. I didn't know how to handle the pressure of being a young wife with a young husband who preferred getting high and causing problems over spending quality time with me. I wanted him to be the same person I had dated. Consequentially, my suicidal thoughts and depression were aiding my addiction to dysfunction.

CHAPTER 12

Awareness: Chaos in the Streets

Antoine talked me out of my suicide attempt by promising that things would get better, and they did for a short period of time. One day while he was visiting a local park near the navy hospital, he ran into Mike who was an acquaintance from the navy. They became engaged in a heated argument that stemmed from an unresolved incident some weeks earlier. Their argument became physical as the crowd of people surrounded them to fuel the drama. When Mike started to feel threaten, he fled the scene on foot. As Antoine chased him, he jumped into his vehicle and attempted to get away. Antoine and some of his friends jumped into our vehicle and were soon in hot pursuit of him. One of Antoine's friends remembered that he carried a handgun and begged him to use it. His friend just wanted to scare Mike, but in the midst of all the confusion, he grabbed the handgun from the glove box and began firing some shots toward Mike's vehicle. Mike was scared to death, so he frantically steered his vehicle through the traffic while attempting to dodge the bullets that were being fired in his direction. He was finally able to elude them.

Mike went directly to the police department to file a formal complaint against Antoine. In the days that following the incident, the police showed up at our condo to question him. I was completely in the dark and had no idea why they were at our door.

"Are you Antoine?" they asked.

"Yes, I am," he answered.

"We need you to step outside please," they told him.

He accompanied them outside for questioning. He was very naïve and didn't realize that they were interrogated him for a crime. He cooperated with them without the presence of legal counsel thus incriminating himself in his involvement in the incident. After a brief interrogation, one the officers knocked on our door requesting that I give him Antoine's handgun. I was naïve too and went to get the handgun as requested, unaware that they were collecting evidence. I cooperated because I didn't want him to get into any more trouble than he already was in. At that moment, my entire world was turned upside down when the officers carted him off to jail. He was charged with firing a weapon into a dwelling and causing reckless endangerment to another individual.

Mike was ready to prosecute him to the fullest extent of the law, and the prosecutor's office was ready to join him to make sure that happened. I frantically attempted to get in touch with Mike. I was able to find his contact information in Antoine's things, since they had been good friends prior to their disagreement.

I called him right away, "Mike, I need you to drop those charges," I pleaded.

"I refuse to. They tried to kill me, and I was scared to death. Why are you defending him?" he asked.

"I have no choice but to defend him. His behavior was wrong. I'm sorry, but we haven't been married that long, and I can't have my husband going to jail. Please help me," I begged.

After about an hour of pleading and what I will refer to as my best negotiations tactics, Mike agreed to drop the charges. Antoine was released from jail later that evening. We resumed our lives as a young married couple, but in the days that followed, I began to wonder what I had gotten myself into. The entire incident with Mike was very unsettling to me.

About two weeks later, Antoine assumed that things had died down with the police and he wanted his handgun back. He told me that he was planning on going downtown to the police station to ask for it. I warned him that I didn't think it was such a good idea and strongly advised him to leave well enough alone. However, he was determined to retrieve his handgun, so I agreed to accompany him to the police station. Once we arrived, an officer directed us to the property room, but after learning why he was there, he quickly advised us to leave the building.

"Your chances of getting that handgun back are slim to none," the officer advised him.

We left the police station, unaware that the State of California would later pick up the charges against him.

CHAPTER 13

Awareness:
Dreams Fading Fast

Prior to meeting Antoine, I was pursuing a career as a California Highway Patrol Officer (CHP). I had previously completed the majority of the requirements for the position with the exception of the final interview. It seemed like months had passed since I had completed those requirements, and I was still waiting for an invitation to be interviewed. Final interviews were only given to the applicants who were being considered for hire. Once hired, those candidates were sent to the cadet training program at the police academy in San Francisco, California.

I finally received the letter I was waiting for and carefully opened the envelope to read its contents. It stated that I had been selected as a candidate for a final interview. I was so excited! The ideal of finally reaching my career goal to become a CHP was very exciting. I followed the instructions and called right away to make an appointment, and the lady on the other end of the line gave me a time and date to be interviewed. She also provided me with additional instructions, requesting that I bring my husband along with me on the day of my interview. I wore a conservative dress and hoped to successfully pass my interview with flying colors.

When we arrived at the State Police facility for my interview, I was taken into a separate room while Antoine was asked to remain in the lobby. Everything seemed normal. I was seated in front of two gentlemen who were waiting to interview me. The interview began with a series of open-ended questions regarding my qualifications for the position. I answered several of them, but then the line of questioning changed.

Suddenly, I was being questioned about my husband, and they drilled me for information, "Where does your husband work? How often does he indulge in drugs, and how is he able to purchase drugs without a job?" I was humiliated and confused. I didn't understand what my husband's behavior had to do with me qualifying for the position in question, and I began to cry.

"Am I really being considered for the position?" I asked him.

His line of questioning changed again, and he placed the focus back on me.

"Have you smoked marijuana?" he asked me.

I didn't want to incriminate myself since my passing this interview was crucial in determining if I got my dream job, so I hesitated to answer.

"We know that you smoke marijuana. We found some traces in your urine from the sample you supplied," he reported.

"I don't smoke marijuana, but I tried some on New Year's Eve with my husband," I pleaded.

What happened next proved to be the most humiliating day of my life, and I was caught off guard with no awareness as to how this situation had spiraled out of control.

The interviewer called an officer into the room. He advised me that I was under arrest for an unpaid firecracker violation I had received some months earlier. I was devastated. It seemed that my dreams of becoming a California Highway Patrol Officer were fading away right before my eyes. I couldn't believe what was happening to me as the officer read my Miranda rights and handcuffed me. I was going to jail in my conservative dress and high heel shoes. All I could think about was how I had been a good girl all my life. I had never even been suspended from school. It broke my heart to know that I would have an arrest record for something so ridiculous.

The officer escorted me out of the room in handcuffs. As I was being led down the hall, I noticed several police officers outside searching our vehicle. They even called in a K-9 drug unit to the scene. The officers were searching our vehicle for drugs. I was taken outside. I believe they wanted to further humiliate me by making me watch as officers tore our vehicle apart. Antoine was taken outside, too. The officers were able to retrieve a small amount of marijuana that he had left in the glove box prior to entering the building. Inevitably, he was arrest too. I was so embarrassed. Our vehicle was impounded while we were being carted off to jail in two separate police vehicles.

Prior to being placed in the police car, the interviewer walked over to me and attempted to make me feel better by telling me that during the course of their background investigation, they were able to learn a lot of great things about me. Unfortunately, his admitting this was no consolation prize! The information didn't make me feel any better. I was twenty-three years old, and up to that point I had never been in trouble a day in my life. The sad thing about the entire situation was that I was being arrested for a crime I never committed.

On the day in question, I had received a firecracker violation but had never even lit one firecracker. Using fireworks within the city limits of San Diego was illegal, but I was only a spectator of the Fourth of July firecracker display. When the office on foot patrol approached me, I didn't run like the others. I decided not to run since I hadn't committed a crime, but the officer didn't believe me when I told him I wasn't doing illegal fireworks, and he ticketed me anyway. The only thing I was guilty of was not going to court to contest the ticket and for never paying the fine. Consequentially, a warrant for my arrest was issued. I was penalized for my husband's behavior, which disqualified me from ever becoming a California Highway Patrol Officer. When I arrived at the county jail, I was placed in a holding cell. I prayed that they wouldn't require me to undress and change into the jail jumpsuit. Luckily for me, I was released after a few hours.

The jail clerk who prepared my release papers provided me with some great advice that day, "Make sure the next time you come to jail that you come for something worth the visit," she said.

I certainly agreed with her sentiment. Despite all our problems, I remained committed to Antoine, but I secretly blamed him for the entire situation. We continued to live our lives, but the repercussions from his rebelliousness began to take a toll on our marriage. Antoine received notification in the mail that the State of California was picking up the charges against him in the handgun case. The State of California was willing to provide him with a unique proposition that read: *You are required to leave the State of California. You must return to New Jersey immediately. If agreed, the State of California will drop the charges against you. You will not be permitted to return to the state.*

Antoine couldn't believe that the state was picking up the charges against him, but he was relieved that they were providing him with a deal. He refused to incriminate his friend as being the shooter in the incident since he honored their friendship. The fact that the state wasn't going to prosecute him was great news. He agreed to the state's deal. His good fortune was great for him but troublesome for me. I had quite a dilemma and a big decision to make. Relocating meant that I had to leave my mother, my best friends, and quit my job at the San Diego Zoo where I had worked for five years. I was on the fast track and was being considered for future positions in upper management, so I was going to have to give up a lot. I wanted to honor my marriage vows since I strongly believed in them, so I made plans to leave San Diego with Antoine.

CHAPTER 14

Awareness: Pack Up! It's Time to Go!

The thought of moving to Newark was intriguing. I had never experienced snowy winters. In fact, I had never even seen snow. I was excited about being able to visit New York City, too. My father still lived in Brooklyn, and I longed to see him and hoped that my moving to the East Coast would allow us the opportunity to establish a better relationship. Antoine and I made plans to travel from San Diego to Newark by vehicle. We faced a lot of dilemmas; the first was that we were behind on our car payments. It was very possible that our vehicle could be repossessed before we even had the opportunity to leave town. The second dilemma was the size of our vehicle. It wasn't big enough to carry our life's belongings and tow a trailer behind it. The weight from everything would certainly slow us down significantly, thus making the trip very difficult.

We took our chances and decided to deal with each issue as deemed necessary. We finalized our business in San Diego and said our goodbyes to friends and family. My mother really didn't want to see me go, but she gave me her blessings. It was bittersweet leaving

San Diego. I had lived there since I was four years old. I had a keen awareness that my decision to leave was going to be life changing. As we traveled through the California Mountains, the altitude proved to be too much for our vehicle. We were facing our first dilemma head on. It was apparent that in order for us to make it through those mountains that we needed to discard half our life's belongings onto the side of the road. We tearfully tossed them out to reduce the weight of the vehicle. It was devastating for us to watch as people jumped out of their vehicles to claim our life's possessions.

Once we lessened our load, it was smooth sailing during the rest of the trip; that is… until we reached the State of Ohio. As we traveled through Ohio, we ran into a dilemma we had not anticipated. We had a car accident after pulling off the highway onto a dark road. I lost my bearings as I attempted to make a U-turn to get back on the highway. As I turned the steering wheel sharply to the left, the trailer swung around and hit our vehicle, leaving a significant dent in the left-side driver's door panel.

Antoine lashed out at me and began criticizing my driving skills, "It's your fault we got in this accident," he asserted.

"I can't help it that we missed our exit. It's both our fault," I barked back.

He blamed me for getting lost and damaging our vehicle. We were both stressed out from the long trip across country. I attempted to defend myself, which only intensified things, and I was surprised to see how angry Antoine became with me. I didn't understand his antagonism — it was only an accident! For the first time in our marriage, I found his rage toward me to be intimidating. I began to regret leaving San Diego.

Once we made it to Newark, we had to determine where we were going to live until we could secure a place of our own. Initially, we stayed with Antoine's sister Diane and her family. She was very nice and didn't seem to mind the imposition of our brief stay. We helped out by taking care of their children and preparing some of the family meals. Our first few months in Newark were filled with a lot of great memories.

We traveled to New York City by the PATH train frequently. Being on the East Coast was very magical and exciting for me, as I loved being introduced to the sights, the sounds, and the different cultures. The food and shopping were amazing and lived up to all the hype I had heard about it. I had to make some adjustments in the way I carried myself. I had to be vigilant in ways I had not previously been to avoid dangerous situations such as being robbed or having my vehicle stolen.

It wasn't very long until the reality of having to find jobs kicked in. It also didn't take long for our first dilemma to manifest. The repo man found our whereabouts, and our vehicle was repossessed in the darkness of the night. We found ourselves suddenly relying on public transportation to get where we needed to go. I was able to secure a great position through an employment agency at Liberty Mutual Insurance Company as a Claims Representative. I was happy to secure such a prestigious position with a great company. I noticed that most of the young Black women who were around my age were hired as file clerks and typist, and it felt good that I was able to secure a different role. I loved my position and excelled at it.

After working there for a few months, I learned that the company planned to relocate to Parsippany, New Jersey. I didn't have adequate transportation to relocate with them, and Parsippany was very far from Newark. During that time, I also learned that I was pregnant.

I told my boss, "John, I'm not going to be able to relocate with the company. I don't have transportation, and I've just learned that I'm pregnant."

"You've done an excellent job for us. I really hate to see you go, but I understand. Congratulations on your pregnancy," he said.

Needless to say, my employer was not very happy with me, but I had to do what was best for myself. I was very excited to be pregnant. This time I wasn't going to allow any obstacles to prevent me from becoming a mom. Antoine wasn't happy once he learned that we were having a baby, and, in fact, he refused to talk to me for a couple of days. I was devastated and didn't understand his objections. We had been married for nearly three years, but he didn't want a lot of children. I guess we should have had that conversation prior to getting married. I wanted children, well... at least two, so I didn't care what he thought. I was having our child — period!

We moved out of Diane's house to live rent-free in Antoine's ex-brother-in-law's apartment in the housing projects. He wanted to live with his girlfriend in a nearby house, so we took him up on his offer. I enjoyed being pregnant and didn't experience many problems. As time grew closer to my delivery date, my water broke when I got out of bed to go to the bathroom. I thought I just needed to relieve myself, but as I walked toward the bathroom, I felt a gush of water running down my legs that wouldn't stop.

"Antoine, it's time. I think my water just broke!" I yelled.

"I'll grab your stuff! Let's go!" he exclaimed with excitement.

We quickly gathered my belongings for my hospital stay and headed for the hospital on foot. The hospital was literally only a few blocks away, but my contractions began to grow stronger so we flagged down a cab. It took a few minutes for one to finally stop. We instructed the driver to rush us to the hospital. When we arrived, I was admitted immediately and assigned to a room. I was prepared for childbirth, and after being in labor for about twelve hours, I delivered a healthy seven-pound, four-ounce baby boy who we named Rasheed. I was so excited to hold my baby boy in my arms. He was my pride and joy, and I spent countless hours singing and talking to him. I noticed that Antoine was also very happy, and for once we had something positive to focus on in our marriage. We were proud parents with a baby who depended on us to provide a good life for him. I continued working at a job I had secured while I was pregnant, and we enrolled our baby in a local daycare once he was six weeks old so we could both work to support our wants and needs.

A few months after our baby was born, Antoine's ex-brother-in-law wanted to move back into his apartment. It certainly wasn't a good time for him to change his mind. We'd just had our baby, and because of his abrupt decision, we were going to be temporarily homeless. Antoine called his sister, Suzie, to ask if we could stay with her for a while. She lived in another housing project on the other side of town. She had four children and lived in a small three-bedroom apartment that was already cramped. Suzie liked to have a lot of company going in and out of her apartment and there was absolutely no privacy. We were in no position to complain, but after staying at her apartment for a while, we realized that it was not the best fit for our family. A lot of family drama between Antoine and his siblings ensued from us living there. His sister, Diane, was upset that we hadn't asked her if we could return to live at her house. The situation caused us a lot of tension, so we decided that it was time to secure our own place.

Six months following the birth of our son, I found out that I was pregnant again. When I revealed the news to Antoine, he was adamant about me having an abortion. We were already struggling to take care of ourselves and our son. I was very upset that we had not taken any precautions to protect me from getting pregnant. The idea of aborting yet another child was troublesome for me. I believed that there was no excuse for us to get rid of the child we had created. However, I did not have the wherewithal to take up the fight with him to defend our unborn baby. Sadly enough, I caved in and terminated my pregnancy. This would be the second time in my life that I made the choice to cave in to the wants of my mate over the valuable life of a child that God had given me.

We were living a reckless life, and I found it difficult to be a responsible adult while being married to Antoine. He was capable of securing a fulltime job, but he never seemed to keep one long term. Finances were always tight for us. It was a normal occurrence for us to frequent the local pawnshops to obtain money for our valuables just to get by. We became so desperate that we pawned my wedding ring for a temporary loan and never got it back. I was devastated. I felt like I didn't deserve to have any of the great things that marriage promised to offer me, so I continued to work to financially support our family.

CHAPTER 15

Awareness: Left Without a Place to Go

We eventually got evicted from our apartment after we got behind on our rent payments. For the second time in our marriage, we were homeless with a child. There was no easy solution for our dilemma, and this time we were out of options and left without a place to go. Antoine contacted his estranged father who lived in their family home that had once belonged to his grandparents before they died. Antoine had grown up in the home with his grandparents.

"Dad, is there any way me and my family could stay with you for a while?" he asked him. "We've been evicted."

"I don't have any available apartments, and I'm living in the basement," he told him.

"Dad, I'm desperate. We have no other place to go," he pleaded.

"Let me get back with you," he said.

After some consideration, he granted us permission to temporarily live in the unfinished basement with our child. We were so desperate that we took his offer immediately.

For me this was certainly a new low. While growing up, my mother didn't have a lot of money, but we never lived in such substandard conditions. Antoine and I had to swallow our pride while living in the unfinished basement, but it was certainly better than being homeless. It was a humbling experience. The unfinished basement was drab and gloomy, and there were a lot of the family's belongings stored down there. I wasn't sure what to expect. I didn't know if there were rodents down there, so I had to keep my fingers crossed and hoped I didn't see any. We roped off a section big enough for our bed and a small amount of belongings. We hung some sheets up so that we could have some privacy when getting dressed. There was running water available, but there wasn't a toilet or a place to bathe, so we had to wash up in the big basin sink. We went up to the first floor apartment when we needed to relive ourselves. We kept a low profile, only coming and going as necessary, but we made weekly trips to the grocery store. During one of those trips, we were robbed at gunpoint in broad daylight.

"Give me that jacket, punk," the thug demanded.

I was terrified. The thug wanted Antoine's brand-new leather jacket. It was common to get robbed for clothing items, jewelry, shoes, and other things of value.

The thug shoved a gun in Antoine's face, "I said hurry up and give it to me!" he shouted.

Antoine quickly cooperated with his demands. The thug asked me if I had any money. I told him a very convincing lie that we were already homeless. There was no way I was going to give our last little bit of cash to him. The thug hit Antoine in his jaw and he fell to the ground, as the thug jumped into a nearby waiting vehicle and fled the scene. It was a very traumatic experience, being robbed at gunpoint in front of our two-year-old son. I thanked God that the thug didn't shoot us.

After a couple of months passed, Antoine's father told him there would be a vacancy. The tenant who lived in the second floor apartment was moving out. It was great news! His father said that it was possible we could move out of the unfinished basement into the apartment. His father was living in the first floor apartment with his aunt. I suspect that he felt guilty knowing that his son was living in an unfinished basement with his family. It is possible that he also felt guilty for being absent for the majority of his son's life. His father extended us an offer to move into the second floor apartment and pay a minimal amount of rent.

I was happy to be moving out of the unfinished basement. It was certainly a blessing. We moved into the second-floor apartment right away and were happy to have a real home again. The second floor apartment was spacious and had three bedrooms, a bathroom, kitchen, a dining room, and a pretty-good-sized living room. I could image that once the apartment was fully furnished it would have great style. However, we couldn't afford to furnish it. We only had enough furniture to furnish two of the bedrooms.

Despite our situation, we made certain that our son never went without. He had a playroom full of toys and enjoyed being read to. Our world revolved around him. By the time he was a year and a half old, we noticed that he was showing signs of being intellectually gifted. We always kept him stimulated mentally by reading him books, introducing him to school-aged curriculum, and encouraging him to play his Nintendo gaming system. He seemed to enjoy playing the games, and when he was only two years old, he was able to use a handheld remote to play them just as well as kids three times his age.

We delighted in providing him with nice things. I made a lot of sacrifices to ensure that he was well cared for. One of those sacrifices was being a homebody. I hardly ever spent any money on myself after he was born. Antoine made some sacrifices too, but there was one thing he refused to sacrifice — and that was marijuana. He smoked marijuana daily and would take some risk to purchase it. He liked having a week's supply on hand and got the best deals on marijuana from New York. Antoine went to some of New York's most notorious neighborhoods to purchase a sandwich size bag of marijuana. I worried about him when he went out to purchase it. It really didn't bother me that he smoked marijuana, since it seemed to keep him calm and happy. I did insist that he not smoke it around our son, and he honored my request.

Antoine and his mother had a dysfunctional relationship, mostly because she had been an absentee parent. She had abandoned him when he was a baby and left him in the care of his paternal grandparents. She'd chosen a life of drugs over her children. When we returned to Newark, he saw his mother occasionally out in the streets.

During one of those sightings, his mother revealed to him that she didn't have long to live, "I've contracted HIV Aids," his mother reported.

The news of her imminent death didn't seem to impact him. He really didn't know her and found it hard to feel sorry for her. The only close connection they shared was with her eleven-year-old son. Antoine's younger brother lived with their maternal grandmother and would visit our home frequently to play video games with his little nephew.

CHAPTER 16

Awareness: The Twins Who Changed My Life

S hortly after his mother died, I found out that I was pregnant again. Just like the times before, Antoine's first reaction was anger. He wanted me to have another abortion. I was not surprised by his reaction. Having an abortion seemed to be our preferred method of birth control, but having the procedure affected me emotionally. I certainly didn't want to force any more children on Antoine that he didn't want, so I begrudgingly agreed to have the procedure. I made an appointment to terminate my pregnancy and was given an appointment time and date to come to the hospital. The clerk informed me that I needed to come the day before the procedure to have some blood work and have an ultrasound completed. I went to the hospital the day before with Antoine and our son.

When we arrived at the hospital, I was taken into a room to have my ultrasound. During the exam, I noticed that the technician continued to rotate the device over my abdomen. She had a concerned look on her face. Her actions caused me some immediate concern. She left the room and returned with another technician. They studied the monitor as one of them rotated the device over a certain part of my abdomen. Neither one of them said a word, which made me wonder what was wrong. At that moment, God whispered to my spirit to reveal that there were two babies growing inside of me. I asked the technicians if everything was all right. Both of them kept poker faces and instructed me to get dressed.

"Is there something wrong?" I asked them.

They continued to keep quite, but their actions spoke volumes, and I knew that I wouldn't be returning the next day for my procedure. As I got dressed, God repeated the same promise again to my spirit. He was letting me know that this time I was being tested. He had given me two babies and wanted me to trust in Him enough to know that He had plans for their lives and that I was just the vessel. At that point, I knew I had to have courage. There was no way I could live with myself if I aborted twins. I considered what a blessing it was to be able to have twins. I was so grateful that God had not punished me for my past actions.

I walked back to the waiting area where Antoine and our son were.

"We're having twins," I said.

"Were not having twins," he replied.

I told him about my experience in the ultrasound room. I told him that I was positive we were having twins. He was shocked and couldn't believe it was even possible, although Antoine did have a couple of sets of twins in his family. I told him that there was no way I could terminate my pregnancy and took a firm position with him. This time things were going to be different. I wasn't going to allow him to talk me out of having our twins. I wanted him to be confident in the revelation I had received from God, so I decided to take a bold approach. I walked up to the clerk's desk with Antoine.

"Can you please tell me if I'm having twins?" I pleaded.

She confirmed my suspicions by not saying a word, but she gazed into my eyes for a few seconds and nodded her head. Antoine observed my encounter with her.

"I won't be back tomorrow," I announced.

Our young family was expanding. Surprisingly, Antoine began to welcome the news. He was happy that we were having twins. It was July 1988; I worked at my job until my doctor forced me to be on bed rest. She advised me that I would be admitted into the hospital until I gave birth to my twins. The idea of staying in the hospital for nearly six weeks didn't make me happy. I notified my employer that I was going to begin my pregnancy leave immediately. My employer was caught off guard, since he believed that I would be able to work for at least one more month. I apologized for my abruptness and reminded him that it was the doctor's orders.

I packed my bags and checked myself into the hospital as ordered. After being there for about a week, I began to feel anxious and didn't know how I could possibly stay there for five more weeks. My doctor ordered an Amniocentesis test to see if my twin's lungs were developed. She wanted to determine if she could schedule a cesarean section. The Amniocentesis test requires the use of a large needle to extract fluids to be tested to determine the development of the child's lungs. I saw this test as a way to get out of the hospital and put a plan of action in place. After the Amniocentesis test was completed, I began jumping up and down several times in my room to make my water break. I envisioned the procedure being the equivalent of inserting a pin into a balloon full of water. *Balloons generally pop after a pin has been inserted.* Surprisingly, after I did all that jumping, my water broke. Later that night, I delivered my twins by cesarean section. I didn't know the sex of the babies prior to delivering them and hoped to have twin boys, but Antoine and I were blessed with a beautiful boy and girl. We named our twins Anne and Kashif. They were born six weeks premature and were required to spend a few weeks in the Neonatal Critical Unit. Their doctor had some concerns about the development of their lungs, which wasn't surprising. I had to drag my utility pole down the hall daily just to see my twins while enduring the pain from my cesarean section.

About two weeks later, we were able to bring our beautiful twins home. We really had our hands full with three young children. We didn't have any outside help with them, which made things difficult. I was very excited about being their mother, and despite Antoine's love affair with marijuana, he was a very good father. He loved our three children and really rose to the occasion to do whatever he could to help with their care. I went back to work once I recovered.

Antoine and I had reverse roles in our home; he cared for the children during the day while I worked outside the home. When I returned in the evening, we switched roles. He resumed his daily regimen of smoking marijuana and would often leave our home to hang out with others who had the same habit. I spent a lot of late nights worrying about him when he was away. After three in the morning passed, I would peer through the living room window for hours, wondering where he was. I cried so much that I didn't have any tears left, but I pushed through the tears and continued to take care of our family.

CHAPTER 17

Awareness: Why Does Marriage Have to be so Hard?

I wondered why my marriage had to be so hard. It was the true picture of dysfunction and certainly different than I had imagined it should be. A few months after our twins were born, Antoine's father moved back into the unfinished basement. I suspect he needed his privacy. He indulged in drugs too; his drug of choice was cocaine. We were awakened one morning to learn that he was found dead in the same unfinished basement that we had once called home. His father's death had been caused by a heart attack that resulted from smoking cocaine. His autopsy revealed that his heart busted from ingesting too much. Antoine's father's death meant that we would inherit their family home.

We transitioned from being homeless to becoming homeowners and quickly realized that it was going to be a big challenge. Antoine's great aunt, who lived in the first floor apartment, became upset about his inheriting the home. She had supported his father financially in maintaining it and had kept it out of foreclosure. She believed that she was entitled to the family home. We learned that there was a lot of debt and liens attached to the property, but we were in no financial position to bring the mortgage payments current and certainly didn't have the money to erase the debts. We met with the family attorney who was already involved with taking care of the financial matters, and she secured a buyer and finalized the legalities of the sale. Once all the debt was settled, Antoine received the monies that were left.

It was May 1990; my mother called to notify me that my grandfather had died. I was devastated. He was my absolute favorite person in the world, even though I didn't see him regularly. He was the only living grandparent I had. He had always been nice to me. When I graduated from high school, he sent me a savings bond which really meant a lot to me. I suddenly found myself without any grandparents. My mother told me that she would be traveling to St. Louis to bury her father. I thanked her for notifying me and told her I wouldn't be going. It seemed like there was death all around me.

Antoine and I were faced once again with having to find a place to live. However, since we had benefited financially from the sale of his family home, we were in a better position to secure a place to live. Antoine spent some of the money to purchase a nice vehicle, and we signed a lease on a two-bedroom condo. The money he received disappeared quickly. Antoine continued to smoke marijuana, but he secured a construction job that paid weekly. We didn't have any options other than to both stay employed to meet our $800 a month rent obligation.

A few months after Antoine's father died, I began to feel miserable again. All of the problems we had faced over the years were finally taking a toll on me. I felt like leaving my marriage.

I decided to discuss my feelings with Antoine, "We seem to continue to be moving backwards, and I'm not sure if I want to stay married," I revealed.

82

He didn't take the news too well. He told me he wanted to do whatever it took to keep our young family together. I was frustrated because there were no guarantees that things would ever change. I felt like I deserved a better life than the one I had. I decided to give Antoine the opportunity to save our marriage. Our children were the only positive thing we shared, and we both loved them deeply. I realized that they needed their father, and I decided it was a good reason to fight to make things work.

CHAPTER 18

Awareness: D.O.A on a Harlem Sidewalk

About a month after I shared my feelings with Antoine, he was murdered on Friday 13, 1990. He had gone to work at his construction job that day and returned home early. Antoine told me that he planned to go to the housing project to visit his uncle and his sister, Suzie. I really didn't mind him going to visit his relatives, since he had not seen them in a while. I kissed him goodbye and he left. I had no idea that it would be the last time I would ever see him alive. In his absence, I played with our three children. Around 5:00 P.M. that evening, I heard a knock on the door. It was unusual for anyone to be knocking, since we rarely had company. I answered the door, and I could tell by the look on the person's face that they had come to bring news that would change my life. It was Antoine's sister, Suzie, and she was crying.

"Antoine was shot in Harlem; we need to go over there right now," she said.

"In Harlem? What was he doing over there?" I questioned.

"I don't know, but come on; lets go," she stated with urgency.

She went on to tell me that he and his two friends were shot a few hours earlier in Harlem. I was consumed with anger. My first thought was, *Here we go again. Now we have one more problem to deal with.* I wasn't even aware that Antoine was going to New York that day. I gathered our three children and headed out the door with Suzie to her apartment in the housing projects.

When we arrived at Suzie's apartment, we were provided with more details about what had transpired earlier that day from one of Antoine's friends who had escaped the ordeal without injury. His account of the facts was being repeated all over the housing projects. We learned that Antoine and his two friends had traveled to Harlem on the PATH train. When they arrived, they decided to do some window-shopping while they enjoyed the hot summer day. Antoine loved to go window-shopping. He loved sneakers and always stayed current on the new releases for each season. They decided to take a shortcut through one of Harlem's housing projects. As they walked to their destination, they shared stories while barely paying attention to their surroundings. Antoine and his two friends thought they heard some gunshots but assumed that the gunshots were random. It wasn't unusual to hear gunshots in the projects, but they had no idea the shots were being aimed at them. As the gunshots rang out loudly in the open air, they were accompanied by a lot of yelling in Spanish. Antoine and his friends noticed two Dominican young men running toward them. At first they continued walking, but the yelling seemed to get louder. The two Dominican young men began firing more shots. Antoine and his friends fled the scene while attempting to find safety. They ran in different directions to escape the mayhem, but Antoine and Kenny found themselves facing the two Dominican gunmen. They were both shot at close range and left to fend for themselves.

Once we took in the sordid details of the day, Kenny's mother Donna took Suzie and me to Harlem to see our loved ones in the hospital. The car ride from Newark to Harlem seemed like it took forever. Once we arrived in Harlem, we went to the nearest hospital we could find. Donna parked her vehicle, and we quickly entered the first Harlem hospital we stumbled upon. Donna learned that Kenny had been admitted earlier.

"Is Antoine here too?" I asked.

"I'm sorry; we don't have anyone here by that name. It is possible that he was transported to another nearby hospital," she said.

With my bad news in hand, we rushed down the hall to Kenny's room to see him. He was lying in his hospital bed hooked up to various monitors. His nurse reported that he had been shot in the back and had recently undergone surgery to remove the bullet, but his doctor had decided not to remove the bullet since removing it could have caused him to be permanently paralyzed. We were surprised to find Kenny alert. He seemed relieved to see his mother. I could tell he was still in a lot of pain. The nurse told Donna that his doctor wanted to talk to her in private. Kenny's doctor advised his mother not to ask him too many questions about the shooting because he didn't want to upset him.

I wanted to interrogate Kenny even though he lay there defenseless. I wanted to know whose idea it was to go to Harlem. I became irritated with him. I assumed that it was his idea, since he sold marijuana and had probably wanted to go to replenish his stock. I wanted to blame him for the entire situation. Since I couldn't get the answers I needed, I was ready to leave his bedside to look for Antoine. I began to have a panic attack as we left the hospital. Donna seemed relieved to find her son in good spirits. He was going to survive. We left his bedside to look for Antoine; Donna assured me that we would go to every

87

hospital in Harlem until we found him. She was very considerate, given the fact that her son needed her too.

We decided to try Harlem Hospital, since it was in close proximity to the one we left. As Donna parked the vehicle, I jumped out, ran inside, and went directly to the information desk and frantically began asking questions.

"Do you have an Antoine here?" I questioned in desperation.

"We do. He arrived by ambulance earlier today," the clerk verified.

She checked the records and gave me his room number. While still in a state of panic, I ran toward the elevator, but before I could push the button, she summoned me back over to her desk.

"Your husband's doctor would like to talk to you. Could you please wait over there in that room?" she requested.

As I walked toward the waiting room, a feeling of sadness consumed my entire body. I attempted to brace myself for the news. In my spirit, I knew I wasn't going to be delivered good news that day, and I nervously awaited the doctor's arrival.

When he entered the room, he immediately asked, "Are you Antoine's wife?"

I answered yes and anticipated what he would say next.

"Me and my team worked really hard this afternoon on your husband," he reported.

That statement was followed with the words that will echo in my ears forever, "I'm sorry. Your husband died on the operating table," he said.

"No! No!" I yelled out hysterically.

I began to sob uncontrollably. The doctor advised me to return to the information desk to collect Antoine's belongings. I was literally in shock and couldn't believe my ears. I stood there paralyzed. Antoine's sister, Suzie, began hollering loudly in the lobby. She was clearly distraught. Donna attempted to comfort me as she escorted me over to the clerk where I collected his belonging. The clerk provided me with additional information about where I needed to go to identify his body. I didn't know what to do or how to feel. After I had all the information I needed, we returned to Newark.

I rode in silence all the way back to Newark. My feelings were all over the place. Just like a yo-yo, they went from anger to blame and from blame to anger in an instant. Kenny was the person I wanted to blame for Antoine's death. I didn't understand how he was still alive and Antoine wasn't. He was the one who took a lot of risks to sell marijuana daily. Antoine did not sell drugs. The only thing he was guilty of was smoking marijuana. I wanted answers and I wanted them now! I wanted to know how a man with a wife and three children could have his life cut short. I found Antoine's death to be very unfair.

By the time we arrived back at Suzie's apartment, the news of his death had spread all over the housing projects. I didn't like all the attention I was getting from his death and felt like I was in the middle of my worst nightmare. I now had three children to care for all by myself. My children were fatherless. I had become a widow at the age of twenty-nine. What made matters even worse was that I had no idea how I was going to bury him. Suddenly, it felt like I was carrying the entire world on my shoulders.

I didn't have time to grieve his death; I had a lot to do. I needed to stay focused so I could take care of all the business matters I was suddenly faced with. It became apparent pretty quickly that I wasn't going to get any financial support from anyone in Antoine's family. No one volunteered to even give me one dime.

The day after Antoine's death, I returned to New York to identify his body at the New York City Morgue. When I arrived, I was taken into a room that resembled the ones often seen on television. His body lay stiff on a long metal table with a white sheet covering it. The attendant at the morgue pulled back the white sheet to reveal his body. I took a deep breath and confirmed that it was him. For some reason, I felt a sense of peace while in his presence. As he lay there on the metal table, he looked the same as he did when he was alive. I was surprised that his body didn't look like it had gone through such a traumatic ordeal. He had sustained fatal shots to his abdomen that caused him to bleed to death on a Harlem sidewalk. I made my peace with him and returned home to Newark to begin making funeral arrangements for him. He had died a young death when only twenty-seven years old.

CHAPTER 19

Awareness:
Running Out of Time

I called my employer to inquire about the supplemental life insurance I had selected when I was a new hire, but the corporate office had never received my forms, and they said there was nothing they could do for me. I didn't know how I was going to prove that I had turned my paperwork in. I called the local office, but they told me that the benefits clerk was on sick leave. I was frustrated and running out of time. I needed to make funeral arrangements for my husband, but I couldn't get anyone in the local office to validate my claim. I needed the money bad. It was frustrating with having to fight an adversary at a time when I needed compassion. I was devastated, and the funeral home was pressuring me to come up with cash. They were not willing to work with me. No payment installments or IOUs. They wanted cash.

I was forced to come up with plan "B", and the only thing I owned of value was the vehicle Antoine had recently purchased. I would have to go without one, since I needed to bury my husband. My best friend Dee came to Newark from San Diego to support and comfort me. I really appreciated her being there for me, since I didn't have any family in Newark. Antoine's older sister Janet also stepped up to do what she could to help. They accompanied me as I went on a mission to sell my vehicle. We went to various car lots, attempting to sell my 1997 Volvo. I decided to take my vehicle back to the dealership where Antoine had originally purchased it. They refused to offer me anything close to what he had paid for it, which was $11,500 dollars. I was furious and couldn't believe that anyone would take advantage of a young widow in her time of need. The Volvo was in "like new" condition, and I was expecting to get at least $8,000 dollars from the sale. I realized how the game was played; they expected me to take a loss while they made a profit from the resale. Initially, I refused to take the ridiculous amount of cash that was being offered to me. I continued to search for a dealership that would treat me with dignity. The more I searched, the more frustrated I became. Every dealership seemed to offer the same amount. They offered $5, 000 dollars, and that was their final answer.

The funeral home would not proceed with the arrangements without a cash deposit. The total cost of the funeral was $3,500, and it was apparent that I would have to accept the $5,000 for my vehicle. I had to redirect my focus and not worry about being ripped off. I sold my vehicle for $5,000 and went directly to the funeral home to finalize the arrangements. They provided me with the times for the viewing and the funeral. I quickly got the word out to Antoine's friends and family who wanted to attend his home going. I went shopping to ensure that his children and I would look our best. The funeral home requested that I deliver the attire that I wanted to lay him to rest in. I buried my husband in a blue suit similar to the one he'd worn when we got married.

As the day of his funeral got closer, my heart ached for my children. They were now fatherless. My oldest son was four and my twins were barely two. The reality that my husband had been murdered in cold blood sank in. My children were too young to appreciate their father, but he had loved them dearly. I continued to stay at Suzie's apartment until the day of the funeral. I lost a significant amount of weight from the day I learned Antoine had died up to the day I had to bury him. I was definitely stressed out.

On the evening of his two viewings, there were droves of friends and family who showed up to say their goodbyes. We had the funeral the next day. It seemed so surreal. I placed pictures of our children and me in his suit coat pocket. I wanted the photos to be buried with him. I did not necessarily believe in spirits, however, a few days before the funeral, a spiritual medium that lived in Suzie's housing projects had pulled me to the side for a talk, "Your husband has a message for you," she announced.

"Excuse me?" I said.

"Your husband didn't want to leave you and your children. His spirit will not rest unless you place pictures in his suit coat pocket," she explained.

"I understand, and I will," I told her.

"Your husband laid on a Harlem sidewalk, left to bleed to death. He knew he was going to die and apologized," she further stated.

I believed her and wanted to make sure his spirit would be at peace, so I did exactly what she'd told me to do.

As soon as his funeral was over, I needed to get away from everyone. I didn't want anything to do with his family. I felt as if they had let me down financially during the days prior to his funeral. I just wanted to go home with my children and vowed never to return to those housing projects again. I gathered our belongings and planned to go home, but prior to leaving, we received a call from the New York City Prosecutor's Office, "The person allegedly responsible for your husband's murder has been apprehended," she reported.

It was a big relief to receive the news. My husband's friends and family who lived in the housing projects cheered when they heard the news. The New York City Prosecutor assured me that Antoine's death had been, in fact, a case of mistaken identity. He and his two friends were simply in the wrong place at the wrong time. The Dominican young men had mistaken them for some other individuals who they had argued with earlier that day. The prosecutor told me that my husband was left to bleed to death on the sidewalk while bystanders watched. No one was willing to call 911. If you lived in the projects, you followed the code of the streets, which was to keep your mouth shut. However, an older woman who lived in the Harlem housing projects eventually called 911. She thought the injured victim on the sidewalk was her son. I received a lot of solace from hearing the details of my husband death from the prosecutor. The prosecutor requested that everyone who was involved in the case attend the trial of the accused murderer of my husband. I told the prosecutor that I wouldn't be in attendance. It would be too much for me. I believed that my husband's killer's trial would be the one thing that would destroy me. I didn't have the courage to face the man who had murdered my husband. I did not want to live with his image imbedded in my memory forever. I had to stay strong for my children. I had no intention of running back and forth to New York for the trial. The prosecutor understood and explained that the accused murderer had a very long rap sheet and would more than likely die behind bars since he was infected with the HIV virus. My priority was to take care of my three children and find housing for us. I cooperated with the prosecutor's office by telephone and provide them with all the information about my husband they needed. I also filed a case with the New York State's Crime Victims Board, since my husband's life had been cut short due to no fault of his own.

CHAPTER 20

Awareness: A Widow's Survival

I returned to the apartment that Antoine and I had shared prior to his death. It was strange being there, knowing that he would never walk through the front door again. I had to push forward through the difficulties of my circumstances, and I had three small children to take care of without any assistance. My best friend Dee had to return to San Diego to her family. I only had myself to depend on. I prepared to return to work, since I needed to keep the money coming in for me and my children. I never even entertained the thought of going on welfare. In theory it seemed like my best option, but I was too proud. I was definitely going to have to take up the issue with my employer for their refusal to pay my claim for my supplemental life insurance. However, I had a bigger challenge to deal with, so I put the issue on the back burner.

I found myself abandoned and left alone to come up with answers about how I was going to pay the $800 a month rent obligation for my condo. I decided to call him and explain my situation, "My husband was murdered, and I will not be able to make my rent obligations," I said.

He was very sympathetic and agreed to allow me time to put a plan of action together. I was under a lot of stress from the entire ordeal; however, God sustained me through my struggles. He showed me His Amazing Grace at every obstacle. I went back to work as planned and confronted the benefits clerk. I wanted answers about how my paperwork had disappeared. I asked her what had happened to my supplemental insurance papers, and she told me that there had been a mistake with processing them. She assured me that she sent them to the corporate office as required and took full responsibility for following up and getting answers for me. Although I knew that she provided me with a true account of her actions, it simply didn't change the fact that I hadn't received death benefits. I decided to take more progressive action against my employer for their blunder. In the meantime, I continue to work for them while I initiated a lawsuit.

A few weeks after Antoine's death, I received a letter in the mail stating that I had been approved for low-income housing. It was perfect timing! Antoine and I had applied for low-income housing and were placed on a waiting list. It had been nearly a year earlier when we put in our application. The letter stated that the low-income housing we were awarded was going to be in one of Newark's most notorious housing projects. The news was certainly a blessing in disguise. I was relieved because the move meant that my monthly rent obligation would be reduced from $800 a month to $250. I could easily afford the lower rent payments; however, I had some concerns about moving into those notorious housing projects. I'd heard stories about them that scared me to death. There was a lot of crime associated with those housing projects. Most of the crime was violence, drug activity, and murder. The most positive thing about living in those notorious housing projects was there was a heavy police presence and security for all the residents.

Regardless, I had to do what was best for my children and myself at the time. I notified the owner of my condo. I told him my good news and provided him with immediate notice of my move date. He was very sympathetic to my situation and offered to do whatever he could to assist me. I didn't have a lot of furniture or possessions to move, so I asked my children's babysitter and her husband to assist me with the move. I made an appointment with the manager of the housing projects to view the apartment and secure the keys, and I noticed right away that the apartment I had been assigned was located in the front of the building. The manager assured me that the Newark Police provided around-the-clock security. God was really watching over me and my children, and it was a blessing to be able to have peace of mind knowing there would be security.

Things were starting to look up for me, and I established a normal routine for myself and my children. I placed them in a local daycare while I went to work. The instructor of my oldest son's class recommended him to be placed in an accelerated learning environment and confirmed that Rasheed was gifted. He was selected to be the valedictorian of his preschool graduating class. I dedicated every waking hour of my time and attention to my children. I was so proud of Rasheed. His graduation ceremony was adorable. The children dressed in caps and gowns. They looked like miniature high school graduates. Later that year, I also learned that I was eligible to receive Social Security (SSI) payments for my children based on their father's Social Security record. Receiving the extra money meant that I wouldn't have to struggle to take care of them. God was really blessing me through my storm. I spent a lot of time with the mother of Antoine's son. His death had brought us closer, and we were like sisters. I informed her about the SSI benefits, and she applied and secured the benefits to help take care of my stepson Jamal.

We were progressing in a positive direction until I ran into an obstacle. During a routine check-up at the pediatrician, I learned that my youngest son had a bilateral hernia in his groin area. His doctor wanted him to have immediate surgery to remedy the situation. I was scared to death to have my son go under the knife, especially when I had just lost his father a few months earlier. Suggesting that I allow someone to operate on my two-year-old son seemed unsettling, and I didn't know if I would be strong enough to go through the process alone. My mind ran through a gamut of thoughts, such as, *What if my son doesn't pull through?*

I prayed to God for strength, and I agreed to allow my son to have the much-needed surgical procedure. He came though his operation with flying colors, even though I had been anxious the entire time he was being operated on. I was very relieved and thanked God that he was okay.

CHAPTER 21

Awareness: New Beginnings in the Lone Star State

As time passed, I started to contemplate moving out of New Jersey. The thought of raising three children alone in Newark terrified me. I wanted to ensure that my children had an opportunity to make a good life for themselves and not become another statistic of the street life. I wanted my sons to become great young men, and I also wanted to raise a confident young woman in my daughter. I realized that living in the housing projects long term would not be an option for me, so I spent a lot of time discussing my options with my mother. She reminded me of some of them. One of them was to relocate to Killeen, Texas with her brother. My Uncle Richard was a decorated military veteran who had made Killeen his home and had a few business connections there. My mother told him about my situation, and then she suggested that I give him a call. The thought of moving back out West was exciting, so I contacted my uncle to learn about the possibility of relocating to Killeen.

The way things were coming together for me seemed so surreal. However, I was still looking for answers and direction. I wanted to make a good decision. One day while I was watching television, I saw a commercial with a psychic who was making predictions about the future for a small fee. I decided to call the number that was provided. It was an 800 number. I knew some people who believe wholeheartedly in psychics. They took their word over God's promises. I found their experiences to be interesting, and I was desperate and wanted to see what my future would hold.

She explained, *"You're going to live in a warm climate, enjoy a long life, live comfortably, meet a man who will resist the idea of being married but will change his mind, and one of your children will be famous."*

I was excited about the information she provided me, and I recorded it on a piece of paper. Her confirmation about my living in a warmer climate was all I needed to go forward with my plans to relocate to Killeen, Texas. My Uncle Richard assured me that the move would be good for me and my children. He extended an initiation for us to live with him for a while. I thought long and hard about his offer and continued to speak to him and his daughter, Mary, frequently about what the city of Killeen had to offer.

"What are the living conditions and the employment opportunities like there?" I asked.

"It's beautiful here. You'll love it," he told me.

I asked him to send me a copy of Killeen's Sunday newspaper to do some research of my own. I was surprised to see how inexpensive the rent was, and I could easily afford the rent for a three or four-bedroom house in an upscale neighborhood. After I had concluded my research, I was ready to make a sound decision. I decided that me and my three children would head to the Lone Star State of Texas.

It was almost a year since my husband had been murdered, and leaving Newark didn't seem to bother me at all. I made arrangements to take a train from Newark to Killeen, Texas. It was going to take two days to make the trip. My children were very excited to travel by train, but the train ride cross-country was uneventful.

When we arrived at the train station, we were met by my Uncle Richard and my Cousin Mary. I was very happy that I would soon be an official resident of Texas, and I was looking forward to the year-round sunny weather. My Uncle Richard arranged for us to live with him in the apartment duplex he owned. I was a little uncomfortable there since he lived with two other people. I realized that our living arrangement would be challenging for me. Although he went out of his way to make us feel comfortable, I still didn't like the idea of living with a lot of people. Prior to moving in with him, I had never depended on anyone. My uncle wanted to take on the role of being my father figure, which didn't make me happy. I certainly didn't need a father at the age of thirty, so I made up my mind to secure my own place as soon as I could. I discussed the possibility of moving into my own place with my uncle. He informed me that one of the apartments in his duplex would be available for rent soon.

"Benita, can you share the apartment with your cousin and her husband?" he asked.

"I don't like that idea, Uncle Richard; they need their privacy as do I," I reported.

I was a single woman with three children, and my cousin was still a newlywed. We all needed our own privacy and space. When the apartment became available, my three children and I moved in. After a few months of living in Killeen, I was able to secure employment with my previous employer from Newark. The company had another office in Austin, Texas. The only problem with accepting the position was that I had to commute daily, and it was a fifty-minute drive each way. I decided to accept the position and make the commute. I enrolled my children in a local daycare in Killeen and purchased some reliable inexpensive transportation, and I began commuting right away.

I decided that it was the right time to secure an attorney to pursue my lawsuit for the supplemental life insurance benefits I had been denied. I knew it would be awkward accepting the new position while also seeking restitution, but my attorney assured me that if we partnered with another law firm who specialized in those types of litigations, we would be successful. I agreed to do so. Approximately six months after filing my lawsuit, I won. The case was settled out of court, and I continued to work for the company. I received a substantially smaller settlement, but I was proud of myself for having the courage to go through with the lawsuit. Winning my lawsuit brought me closure for all the problems I had endured while trying to bury my husband.

CHAPTER 22

Awareness: Soldiers in Disguises

Things were going well for me in Killeen. I considered the idea of dating, and Killeen seemed like a great place to meet single men. I lived very close to the Fort Hood Army Base, so there were plenty of suitors to pick from. I began to receive a lot of attention as I walked around town with my children. The first army soldier I met seemed to be perfect. His name was Mike. He was good-looking, funny, and drove a nice BMW. I was certainly attracted to him. As we got to know one another, he became very comfortable around me. After learning that I was commuting daily to Austin, Mike offered to allow me to drive his car occasionally. I was impressed by his generosity.

"Hey, partner, my car just needs some minor repairs," he informed me, "and you're welcome to use it if you take care of them for me," he offered.

"Wow! I can't believe you're going to allow me to put all those miles on your car," I said.

"Anything for you," he replied.

I thought that the offer was reasonable, since his vehicle was more reliable than mine. I wanted to make sure I had backup transportation, so I paid a couple hundred dollars for the repairs on his car.

One evening, I called Mike to make arrangements to drive his vehicle to work the next day, and he assured me that he would come over in the morning for me to use it. When I awoke, I got dressed. The time that he agreed to come by passed, so I attempted to reach him but couldn't. I was furious. There was no doubt in my mind as to whether he would show up. I drove my own vehicle to work, and when I got off, I drove directly to the base, but I was unable to find Mike. He dodged me for weeks, so I made peace with the fact that I gotten ripped off. I couldn't believe that this was going to be the caliber of men I would have to choose from.

I met a few more soldiers after that and wondered if any of them were worth my time and attention. Most of them were immature, which really turned me off. Those soldiers lied about everything! I found it hard to ascertain what they wanted in a relationship, or even worse — if they were married. I began to find the entire dating scene to be a cumbersome process and began to lose interest. I liked the idea of being in a serious relationship, so I needed to be careful in selecting individuals to date since I had children. I didn't want to bring strangers around them or place myself in any danger.

Over the course of the next six months I went on a few dates, but it seemed like every time I thought I had found *"Mr. Right"*, he turned out to be *"Mr. So Wrong."* I didn't want any more stress or drama in my life, and I began seeing one army soldier who seemed worth my time and attention. His name was Chuck. I started to consider getting to know him on a more serious level and even considered introducing my children to him. One day, Chuck invited me on a group date. He wanted to meet my children so I agreed to go. I thought my children would like him. Chuck planned a nice trip for us to go to a nearby drive-through animal safari.

He picked us up for our planned date on time. We were having a good time, and he seemed to be great with my children. I was impressed by his patience and acceptance of them. He was proving to be a good suitor who I looked forward to getting to know better. On the way home from our date, we decided to stop to get something to eat. As we were waiting inside the lobby for our carry-out order, a woman entered the restaurant. I noticed right away that the woman didn't look happy. She approached us and started sizing me up and down, so I returned the favor.

She approached Chuck. "I need to speak to you in private," she told him.

I had no idea who this mysterious woman was, and after a brief conversation with her, Chuck walked away from her. She began walking toward us while raising her voice in anger.

"Who is that?" I asked him who she was.

"My wife," he said nonchalantly.

"What are you doing with my husband?" she questioned.

"Listen, lady, I suggest you take up your questions with your husband — not me," I remarked.

I was very annoyed and couldn't believe that he had placed us in such a predicament. Before I knew it, she knocked our take-out order of food out of her husband's hands, and food and drinks went flying everywhere. She was certainly making an embarrassing scene.

"Take me home now and never call me again," I chastised him.

As we all walked out of the restaurant toward Chuck's vehicle, his wife followed. She continued to yell at him while making a scene in the parking lot, and she made several attempts to block me and my children from getting into her husband's vehicle. I couldn't believe I had trusted him with our safety. I was perplexed and wondered why he had lied about his marital status. In our earlier conversations, he had indicated that he and his wife were separated. I asked him how his wife would react if she saw him with another woman, and he assured me that they were both seeing other people. I had no reason not to believe him. I certainly didn't appreciate having my children's wellbeing compromised because of his inability to be truthful with me. There was no way I would continue seeing him.

"Drop me off at Ella's; you and your damn wife are crazy," I complained.

I didn't want her to know where I lived, and I continued to look in the side view mirror of his vehicle as he attempted to elude her, but she remained in hot pursuit of him. When I arrived at Ella's house, I quickly jumped out of his car with my children in hand and never spoke to him again.

I stormed into Ella's house and began using some profanity to describe the details of the day. Ella was in disbelief and suggested that we go out to the local VFW club in town. She believed that a night on the town would be just the trick to help take my mind off the day's events. Initially I declined her offer. I certainly didn't feel like being in the company of any more liars who were camouflaged as soldiers in military uniforms, but it was apparent that if I wanted to date anyone while living in Killeen, my only choice would be army soldiers. There were no other options since Killeen is a military town. After some consideration, I decided that some good music and the company of my good friend Ella would be beneficial, so I secured a babysitter, got dressed, and headed out for the night.

CHAPTER 23

Acceptance: Heightened Hottie Alert

When we arrived at the club, I was still distraught from the events which had transpired earlier, but I paid my entry fee and went inside. Two minutes hadn't passed before Ella was on a *"Heightened hottie alert"* and noticed a very attractive, muscular gentleman standing at the bar.

"Look at that fine man over there," she pointed out.

"He *is* pretty cute. Watch this," I said.

He had caught *my* eye, too. I acknowledge that I had seen him and told her that I was going to approach him to see if he wanted to dance. I was feeling pretty self-assured, so that's exactly what I did. I approached him and began making some small talk. During our brief conversation, I asked him to dance. I felt pretty confident that he found me to be attractive, too. In my mind, I believed that there would be no way he would decline my offer, but to my surprise — he did. He attempted to offer me a brief explanation as to why he didn't want to dance. He said that he didn't like the song that was playing. I knew he wasn't being truthful with his answer. The song that was playing was one of the hottest club mixes, but I decided that I wasn't going to permit his rejection to put a damper on my evening. It was his loss! I politely excused myself and ordered a drink.

I moved away from the bar with my drink in my hand and proceeded to find a table for Ella and myself. I quickly forgot about the attractive, muscular gentleman at the bar and began to relax. I enjoyed my tasty drink and the club's atmosphere. Ella and I always had a good time when we went out together. We watched the patrons as they enjoyed themselves. After what seemed to be about an hour, I noticed the attractive, muscular gentleman was standing in a nearby corner of the club. He was attempting to get my attention by gesturing for me to come over to him. I found his hand gestures to be odd. I wondered what he wanted. I was sure that it wasn't to dance. I wondered why he didn't just walk over to my table to talk to me. I decided to go see what he wanted. As I approached him, he attempted to re-direct me over to yet another part of the club, so I followed him. He finally stopped walking once we were in the back of the club.

"What's your name?" he asked me.

"Benita," I answered.

I wasn't in the frame of mind for games, and it certainly seemed like he was playing one. He told me his name was Deon. He went on to say he was new in town and was a soldier in the United States Army.

"How old are you?" I questioned.

"I'm twenty-five, but I'm really mature for my age," he said.

My suspicions were correct; he was six years younger than me. I told him I thought he was too young for me. I had already broken my rule once and dated a younger man, which proved to be problematic and the problems were still fresh in my mind. Deon assured me that he was much more mature than he seemed, so I decided to give him my telephone number. He warned me that he had come to the club with a female friend. He told me that he had met her just within the past week. He tried to convince me that he had simply used her for a ride to the club. I didn't know what to think. I'd heard similar stories from other army soldiers that had proven to be all lies. I instantly labeled Deon as just another army soldier with nothing better to do than spread lies and break female hearts. He returned to his female friend, and I went back to my table. I told Ella about my conversation with Deon. We continued to enjoy ourselves, watch the crowd, and occasionally dance to a song or two ourselves.

When it was time to leave, Deon was standing near the club's entrance with his female friend. We made eye contact while flirting with each other without saying a word. I wanted to send a direct message to him. I wanted to show him that women were also capable of careless flirting. I pinched him on his butt as I disappeared into the darkness of the club's parking lot. I never expected to hear from him again. The next day, I was doing some housework and spending quality time with my children when the telephone rang, so I answered it. Deon was on the other end of the line. He was very soft-spoken and polite, and we engaged in a brief conversation that consisted mostly of small talk.

"Would it be alright if I come over tonight?" he asked.

"I'm going to Walmart with my children," I reported.

"May I call you later?" he replied.

"Please do," I responded.

I encouraged him to call back and provided him with an estimated time to call. He called later that evening just as promised. Deon asked if he could visit me, but he said he didn't have any transportation. He explained that his vehicle was in his home town of Kokomo, Indiana, and that he planned to return home soon to retrieve it. Deon asked me if I had a problem with coming over to the army base to pick him up. My first inclination was that he was really full of himself! For some unknown reason, I didn't believe his story about his vehicle. I figured he probably didn't have one but was too embarrassed to be truthful with me. Nevertheless, I gathered my children and we made the ten minute drive over to the Fort Hood Army Base in my little red Yugo to pick him up.

Deon was waiting outside of his barracks when we arrived. As he entered my vehicle, I checked him out. Deon looked just as handsome as I remembered him and stood about six feet and had an attractive, muscular build. I thought I had died and gone to heaven when I looked at him. He was undoubtedly very good looking. I was glad he had requested to come over so we could get to know one another. He made some small talk with my children during the ride.

When we arrived at my house, I excused myself to get my children ready for bed but quickly returned to the living room where he waited. We spent what seemed like hours talking and getting to know each other. Deon told me that he had recently arrived in Killeen, but prior to that he had been stationed in Germany for a few years and had only been in town for three weeks. Deon was recently divorced and had two children from his marriage. He also mentioned that he had two other children out of wedlock with two other women. I was surprised. He was certainly too young to have four children, but I appreciated the fact that he was so candid about his children and recent divorce. I found his honesty to be refreshing.

The fact that Deon had four children from three different women should have caused me some concern, but I decided to ignore the red flags and just go with the flow, since we seemed to hit it off. When it was time for him to return to his barracks, he called a cab. In the days that followed, Deon wanted to visit me every day. I really didn't mind, since I was enjoying his company, too. He was very sweet to me and surprised me often with nice gifts. Deon brought me pretty dresses that looked very flattering on me. I loved all the gifts that he gave me and appreciated them.

CHAPTER 24

Acceptance: Baggage (The What, Who, When, Where, & How)

After about three weeks of seeing each other, Deon told me that he was expecting a female friend from overseas to visit him. I really appreciated his honesty and couldn't find fault with him since I wanted a man that was a straight shooter. He told me that they had made their plans prior to his meeting me, so I put things in their proper perspective since we weren't a serious couple.

"I hope you realize that you can't come to visit me while you have company," I warned.

"I understand," he chuckled.

Once his female friend left, we resumed our daily visits and began to become a serious item. He had some good qualities and was nice to my children. They seemed to like him, too, which was very important to me. After about three months of dating, we decided to live together. Deon helped me take care of my financial obligations, and it was nice having him around all the time.

We went on a lot of dates. We loved to frequent the batting cages and seemed to have a lot in common. I rallied behind him

111

and encouraged his interests. Deon wanted to pursue his dreams of becoming a musician and a model, and he participated in a few local modeling competitions in Killeen. We had the opportunity to secure some studio time, and he invited me to join him in recording a few tracks for an original song he wrote. I really enjoyed tapping into my creative side, too, and our relationship was building momentum.

After about four months of dating, Deon told me he needed to travel to Kokomo to pick up his two sons and his vehicle. Deon told me his ex-wife Rita had recently been arrested and his children needed him. Deon's mother was caring for them until he could get there. He planned to fly to Kokomo and drive his vehicle back to Killeen. After about a week, he returned with his two young sons in his yellow Cadillac. Deon introduced me to his sons. Marcus was four and his younger brother Terry was two. It was difficult for me to understand how a mother could allow herself to be away from her two young children. Nevertheless, I was more than willing to welcome them and to assist him with their care.

We became an instant family. Our children were very close in age, and Deon's children were very friendly. They seemed to need a lot of attention, but I was more than happy to provide them the attention they needed. We spent a lot of time participating in family activities with our five young children. Some of the activities included going to the park, visiting family-fun places, and playing a lot of family-friendly games. We were all becoming really close. Deon seemed to really appreciate my mothering skills, and we merged our families while continuing to get to know one another. His oldest son, Don, from another relationship, also came to Killeen to visit. He stayed with us for about two weeks. I was having a great time getting to know Deon's children.

After a couple of months, Deon planned to return his children to their mother.

"Would you go to Kokomo with me to take the boys back?" he asked.

"I really want to go, but I don't have anyone to watch the kids," I reminded him.

I really wanted to travel with him, but I had a slight problem; I needed someone to take care of my children. I decided to call my sister who lived in Greenville, Texas to see if she could assist me. She agreed to take care of them and was happy she could help out.

We planned our road trip across country to Kokomo in Deon's yellow Cadillac, and our itinerary included leaving Killeen, stopping in Greenville to drop off my children at my sister's house, and then proceeding northeast to Kokomo, Indiana. We were very fortunate that our five children were still small. Their sizes make it easier for them to all fit comfortably in the back seat of Deon's yellow Cadillac. We secured the children in the vehicle and headed toward Greenville, Texas. My sister was happy to see us when we arrived at her house. After quickly exchanging contact information with her, we got back on the highway but didn't have a lot of time for sightseeing. We needed to drop off his children and get back to Killeen, and our time was limited.

When we arrived in Kokomo, Deon's first priority was to return his children to Rita. He tried to find her but was unsuccessful in his attempts. He decided to go to a few of her friends' houses. When he finally located her, she refused to come out of her friend's house to take their children. Rita's behavior provided me with a lot of insight for things that were yet to come. I was starting to form an opinion about what type of woman and mother she was. At that point, my opinion of her wasn't good. I didn't think she was good at being either a woman or a mother.

Deon made arrangements with his mother and grandmother for us to stay with them while we were visiting. They seemed nice and happy, and they were glad to see Deon.

My first impression of Kokomo wasn't favorable; I thought it was a small backward town. The people were gossipy and nosey, and many of his friends and family weren't shy about letting their opinions be known about him dating. They believed that it was too soon for him to be in a serious relationship after being recently divorced, especially with a woman who had three children. I felt like I was being placed under a microscope while I visited Kokomo. Deon was proud of me and paraded me around like he had just won a first-place ribbon at the state fair, and he did. I was 5'6" and weighed 125 pounds with a slender build. All of his male friends were envious of him when they saw me on his arm.

While we visited, I met his oldest daughter Ty. She lived with her mother, and it was her 8th birthday. Deon wanted to take her shopping at Target to pick out a few things. We seemed to get along pretty well. He also introduced me to Rita's mother June, who was lurking around to see who he was dating. His mother and grandmother maintained a friendly relationship with her. They rented her house, which I thought was a little awkward. It was also odd to me that his mother and grandmother still entertained some of his *"old flames"*. It was uncomfortable having to meet some of them. Kokomo was very different from what I was used to.

Deon showed me around town. I had the opportunity to experience some of the nightlife, which I found to be laughable. Many of the nightclubs were holes in the wall. They were small, dark, and lacked ambiance. They certainly weren't anything like the ones I had frequented in cities like San Diego, Newark, and Killeen. Deon made sure that we spent some time with his two sons during our stay. When it was time for us to travel back to Killeen, we said our goodbyes to his family and children and headed back home to Killeen.

We stopped at Greenville to pick up my children from my sister's house. When we arrived, I thanked her for helping me. We gathered my children and quickly got back on the highway. It felt good to return to normalcy.

My relationship with Deon continued to blossom. We shared my rented three-bedroom house. He was very vocal about his feelings for me. One of the things I liked the most about him was that he told me he loved me every day. He made it clear that he didn't want to have more children, but I understood his sentiment since he already had four of them. I was serious about him, too, but I had a different opinion about having more children. I believed that it would be awkward to be married to someone and not have at least one child with them. I believed that would be a conflict of interest, since we both had children from previous relationships.

When the time came to make a decision regarding reenlisting in the army, Deon didn't want to. He used his medical benefits to have a couple of surgeries, one of which was a vasectomy, which I did support his wishes to do so. I admired the fact that he was taking responsibility to ensure that he didn't have any more children. Deon advised me that he planned to return to Kokomo once his discharge went through. I became bombarded with a lot of information and decisions to make within a short period of time, all of which could be potential deal breakers for our relationship. I had a lot to take into consideration.

Our relationship was on a steady course. We had dated for about for eight months, and we both thought it was time to place some emphasis on the direction we both wanted our relationship to take. We decided to have a serious talk. Deon conveyed that he wanted me to relocate with him to Kokomo, but the next thing he said was earth-shattering, "I want you to go to Kokomo with me, but I'm not going to marry you first," he advised me.

He assured me that he loved me, wanted to be with me, but he needed me to make my own determination if I wanted to go with him or stay there. Here I was, for the second time in my life contemplating whether to follow a man halfway across the country in the name of love. The first thing I needed to consider was my feelings about uprooting my children. We had lived in Killeen for a little over a year, and I thought it might be too soon to move again. I wasn't sure if I wanted to relocate to another state. My children were still young, and we really didn't have any ties to Killeen with the exception of my Uncle Richard. Our relationship was on shaky ground, since I had already severed ties with my uncle because he had spent too much time trying to control me when I lived in his duplex.

I had one school-aged child who was in a gifted kindergarten program, and it was important for me to make sure that Kokomo had similar gifted programs. My second dilemma was to consider the age differences required to start elementary school in the two cities. I didn't want my twins to experience any delays with starting school. I learned that the Kokomo school system's entry age was higher than that of Killeen's, so I considered that to be a negative factor. I questioned whether relocating to Kokomo was worth the risk without having the benefit of a firmer commitment from Deon, and I didn't know how I was going to make the adjustment to the monotonous life Kokomo seemed to offer. I just wasn't sure if I would be happy living there.

The one thing I was sure of was that I loved Deon. I wasn't going to push the envelope by giving him any ultimatums. I'd learned my lesson about trying to force a person to marry me, and I decided to follow my heart. I told him that I was willing to relocate with him and had no expectation of our being married. I was content in knowing that if it was meant for us to get married that it would happen naturally.

"Mama, what do you think about me relocating with Deon?" I asked.

"I don't believe you should go, especially if he isn't going to at least give you a ring," she advised.

My mother thought I needed to remain in Killeen. This time was different; I wasn't desperate to be married like the first time, so I didn't take her advice. We moved forward with our plans to relocate. He had his vasectomy prior to our leaving, because he wanted to seal the deal to ensure that he would never hear another woman murmur the words, "I'm pregnant."

A week before we moved, Deon's younger brother Jay flew out to help us with the drive back to Kokomo. We had two vehicles that needed to be driven, so Jay drove my red Yugo and we went in Deon's yellow Cadillac. We took care of our business by securing school records, military discharge papers, by finalizing the lease on my rented house, and then we packed our belongings into our two vehicles and headed for Kokomo.

We didn't have any concrete plans about where we would stay once we got there, but Deon made tentative arrangements for us to stay with his mother and grandmother. They lived in a small three-bedroom house, so there wasn't going to be a lot of room for the seven of us. When we arrived, we didn't waste any time looking for employment opportunities. Initially, we lived off the small monthly income I received to help us get by.

After about a month of living with his family, we decided to secure a place of our own. I breathed a sigh of relief when we moved. Deon's mother was rude at times. She made it clear that she didn't want me to give her any more grandchildren, "I sure hope you're not pregnant. I don't need any more grandchildren," she said.

I found her comment to be tacky. It was apparent that she had never received the memo that her son couldn't have any more children. That wasn't the last time she uttered sly comments to me. It wasn't any of her business if we decided to have children. I certainly didn't care about what she needed or wanted. I was really turned off by her negative attitude.

The first house we moved into was even smaller than his mother and grandmother's house. We rented a small two-bedroom bungalow, and we were able to make a family chain that allowed us to reach both the front and back doors of the house. The house got even smaller when Deon's children came over to visit.

At first Deon seemed happy to be back in Kokomo, back in his old stomping grounds. He had been born and raised in Kokomo, and the majority of his family, children, and friends lived there. Living in Kokomo was very different for me, since I didn't have any family or friends there, so I wasn't sure if I liked it yet. One of the things I noticed right away was that my children and I were seen as "outsiders". That was the toughest adjustment for me. Nevertheless, I needed to establish a sense of connectivity to Kokomo since it had been my choice to relocate there, and I enrolled my children in the local community daycare.

Deon's ex-wife Rita seemed to be the chief contributor to my dislike for Kokomo. She was against my living in Kokomo with her ex-husband, and she began to cause conflict right away. The first thing she did was make an attempt to destroy Deon's relationship with my children.

"Deon, Marcus says he doesn't like it when those other kids call you Dad," she reported.

When Deon told me about her concerns, I realized that her allegations were certainly ones that were coming from a manipulating woman. Our five children began calling Deon Dad and me Mom when we merged our families in Killeen. Marcus and Terry were the most eager to do so. It was a natural progression for all of them, so they made the choice to call us Mom and Dad. We welcomed their referring to us in that way. I certainly didn't have a problem with my three children calling Deon Dad, especially since they had lost their biological father. Deon was willing to assist me in caring for them. It was apparent that the only person who had a problem with it was Rita. I didn't respect her. It was difficult to understand how a grown woman could be so nasty where children were concerned.

Marcus and Terry were already attending the local daycare where I enrolled my children, and Rita made it clear to Deon that she expected him to take their children to the daycare, especially if he was helping me to transport mine. He had some involvement with transporting my children to the daycare, but I was the primary person who took them daily. Initially I found Rita's request to be reasonable, since we lived around the corner from her. I passed her house daily on the way to the daycare and told Deon that I didn't mind with helping out. One morning, I stopped by Rita's house to pick up the children, and that day she decided to voice her concerns.

"Benita, Marcus doesn't like it when the kids call Deon Dad," she said.

I was in disbelief and couldn't believe that she had the audacity to stick her nose into our business. It wasn't any of her business what my children called Deon. It had nothing whatsoever to do with her. I sternly reminded her that we were going to get married sooner or later.

"Deon will be their step-father. Their real father was murdered, and as far as I am concerned, they can call him whatever makes them feel comfortable," I replied.

I wanted to make certain that Rita understood where I was coming from so we wouldn't have to revisit the issue again. After my conversation with Rita, I realized that living in Kokomo was going to be a bigger challenge than I had expected. I wasn't sure if I could muster up the acceptance for the obstacles I would later face. Deon reminded me that Rita was an instigator who loved to manipulate the people around her. He provided me with many accounts of the anguish she had put him through. Their marriage certainly had been tumultuous. I was able to gain a better insight about the type of woman she was through each of his accounts. I attempted to put things in their proper perspective — so it seemed.

Things between Deon and I were going good. After about six months, we decided to look for a bigger house to accommodate our family, so we secured a nice three-bedroom house and purchased it on contract from a family friend. We appreciated the extra room and especially the large back yard. Our children loved to play outside. The house wasn't in the best part of town, but we felt very comfortable securing a traditional mortgage on it about a year later. We searched for better jobs and set our sights on the local automotive manufacturing plant in town. Deon really wanted to work there. It was his dream job. He had attempted to get on there prior to enlisting in the army. The plant paid excellent wages and provided lucrative benefits, so we began targeting the plant for potential employment opportunities. There were multiple ways to get hired, but the best way was to have a parent who worked there. The program was called the "Sons and Daughters" program.

We didn't have a parent who worked there, making our odds of working there slim, so we contacted the hiring manager several times. Our steadfastness finally paid off. Deon was hired and things improved financially for us. We finally had the freedom to treat ourselves to some of the nicer things in life that we had always wanted. One such purchase was the brand-new white Jeep Deon purchased for me. I was so excited because I had always wanted one.

CHAPTER 25

Acceptance: It's Official— I'm His

It was July 1993; Deon finally asked me to marry him. We were going to make things official. I didn't waste any time letting him know that my answer was a resounding YES! We decided to keep things simple and planned a civil wedding. We picked a date to be married at the Howard County Courthouse. The date we selected was July 23, 1993; however, on July 22, 1993, while we were at the courthouse completing the required paperwork to obtain our marriage license, Deon surprised me by asking me to marry him right there on the spot. I was ecstatic! He surprised the court clerk, too, but she married us right away. It was a special day and certainly a new chapter in our lives.

I was now married for the second time, but I wanted this marriage to be different. We made plans to go on our honeymoon. Deon and I never told a soul that we were married. However, we decided that it was only right to let my children in on the good news. They were very surprised and asked why we hadn't included them in our ceremony. Prior to our getting married, I discussed at length with them the

121

possibility of our getting married. They had granted me permission in advance.

They really liked Deon. He bonded with them and they were comfortable being around him. Having their blessing was very important to me, and I knew that he loved them, too. He was now officially their step-dad, despite anyone else's approval. We extended the news of our union to his family, and it seemed to go without incident. With all the notifications out of the way, we went on our honeymoon to Cincinnati, Ohio. Our itinerary for day one included going to the Cincinnati Jazz Festival, which showcased some of the best R & B artists. Day two included going to Kings Island, a popular amusement park. We had a wonderful time on our honeymoon, although it was too short. The news about our getting married circulated around town pretty quick, and there were a lot of people who weren't happy about our union.

Deon's children continued to visit us every other weekend. We made sure that on the weekends they visited that we planned some fun activities. Some of the activities included visiting nearby kid-friendly attractions, going to the park, and visiting the local skating rink. Our children enjoyed spending quality time together.

Rita seemed to be very jealous once Deon and I were married, and it didn't take long for her to start causing us problems again. She started spreading malicious rumors around town about Deon that weren't true. One such rumor was that he was living the good life with me and paying her the minimal amount of child support that he could. What Rita failed to mention was that he was also ordered to pay support for his other three children. Rita had a very bad habit of acting like she was the only one who had children with Deon. She punished him whenever she felt like it by withholding their children from him, and she limited the amount of time he was allowed to see them. Her antics were beginning to take a toll on him.

Deon's mother was also jealous of Deon's relationship with me. She'd had full control over his finances while he was overseas in Germany, and he relied on her to make purchases for him for his children, pay the bills, and enjoy spending a few dollars every now and then. Once he returned, she was no longer afforded that opportunity, but she still wanted some control. Deon had a new life with me and my children, so she viewed me as a threat. I could tell that she harbored some resentment toward me by her sly negative comments. I tried to ignore most of them, but some were hard to ignore. I didn't understand how she could assume that her adult son would allow her to control him when he was a married adult. I wasn't a threat, and I had my own finances. I complimented her son and made him a better person.

His grandmother was very different, and she really liked me and my children a lot. Deon was well aware of the stressful relationship that existed between his mother and me, but our differences remained the "big elephant in the room" that no one wanted to address.

I encountered a lot of attacks from various individuals simply from being married to Deon. It felt like I was a celebrity who was always under a lot of scrutiny. The attacks seemed to be coming from all directions. Deon's children's mothers joined the bandwagon, too. Somehow, they also believed that I had come to Kokomo to threaten the financial support for their children. My children and I were perceived to be the "bad guys" in the eyes of many. The fact of the matter was, his children's mothers were never interested in legally pursuing the child support that was due them based on the State of Indiana child support guidelines. The main reason why they never sought legal recourse against Deon was because they had been occasionally sleeping with him prior to our meeting. They chose Deon's attention over legally protecting the financial needs of their children, which couldn't be blamed on me.

It seemed like I wasn't going to receive a warm welcome in Kokomo, because Deon's past was haunting me. I did my best to deal with the stress, but I was beginning to feel anxious from all the attacks. Instead of turning to God for comfort and guidance, I allowed the attacks to shake me to the core. I started to feel like I didn't have the wherewithal to counter most of the attacks.

It wasn't very long after we arrived in Kokomo that Deon received notification from the court. He was being summoned for a paternity suit. The court wanted to establish paternity for a child that he had possibly fathered. I quickly learned that Deon was the alleged father of his oldest daughter's sister. I was in disbelief that he had never mentioned the possibility of having another daughter. I felt betrayed. I didn't appreciate having to learn the news that way. The fact that he had kept such important information a secret was certainly a red flag. His dirty little secrets were rearing their ugly heads. By Deon's own account, I learned that he had been a real ladies' man back in the day. As a teen, he had a lot of girls and older women who loved to chase after him, and he'd slept with most of them. I was mortified when he told me. I once heard a saying, "Whoever your partner has slept with, you have also." It seemed like Deon was a real life Kareem Abdul Jabbar. Many women in Kokomo desired his attention, but I couldn't blame them; he is gorgeous.

Deon had married his first wife at nineteen, and by the time he was twenty-one, he had fathered five children. The women who desired his attention didn't seem to care if he was married. He impregnated his oldest daughter's mother while he was still married to Rita. They were pregnant at the same time and delivered their babies within six months of each other. Deon attempted to explain to me how an innocent, little four-year-old girl was made to go so long without the benefit of knowing who her father was. He explained that he wasn't sure if she was his daughter, since he and her mother both slept around a lot. Other men were named as the young girl's father, too. He wasn't going to claim her without the benefit of having a DNA test.

After a few years of avoidance, it was time for Deon to face the music. Most of Deon's avoidance regarding the young girl stemmed from the fact that he had been out of the country in Germany. The state arranged for him to take a DNA test, since they were currently making welfare payments to her mother. It was beneficial for all parties to identify who the young girl's biological father was so that he could assume financial responsibility for her. If Deon was named her father, he would become responsible to pay support. The DNA test can back positive. He was in fact her father and needed to establish a relationship with her. He eventually did the right thing.

Everything about Kokomo started to get under my skin. I went through a lot within a short period of time, and it all seemed so overwhelming. Deon had five children instead of the four. I was constantly being attacked by everyone, and I didn't have any friends to support me. I was transformed into an unhappy camper. Instead of *Sleepless in Seattle,* I was *Miserable in Kokomo.* It was hard for me to find acceptance for that reality! Without friends and family around me, I slowly began to isolate myself. I immersed myself into mothering my children, and I lost the desire to participate in the town's social scene.

After about a year and a half of living in Kokomo, I was also hired by the automobile manufacturing plant. I was thankful that something positive, for a change, was finally happening for me. Our household income doubled. We enjoyed a middle-class lifestyle with all the perks. Being part of the middle class as an adult earner made me feel successful. However, our new success brought even more external problems. It seemed like some of Deon's family and exes were now even more jealous. We tried to ignore most of the jealous rants we heard, either directly or indirectly, and continued to focus on the needs of our immediate family. I began to seek the advice of my spiritual mentor The Winged One. She always encouraged me to look at the situation in big-picture terms. Sometimes I took her great advice, while other times I mindlessly allowed the devil to steal my joy.

Deon's children continued to visit us regularly, and we began to notice that his children were showing signs of distress. Marcus began acting different toward me. It was apparent that his mother was making a great effort to poison our relationship. One day while Marcus was visiting, he started calling me by my first name. I found his behavior to be unusual. He'd begun calling me Mom shortly after he met me in Killeen, so I wondered about the reason for the sudden change. I assured Marcus that it was acceptable for him to call me by my first name if he desired, but I firmly clarified that I wouldn't allow him to call me by my first name one day and Mom the next. I asked him to make a decision right there on the spot as to what he wanted to call me, and he told me his choice was to call me Mom.

CHAPTER 26

Acceptance: Children in Distress

Rita's antics were not surprising. In fact, they were becoming predictable. We really didn't know why his children were in distress. We realized that we needed to look for indicators so we could address their issues. Marcus began to ask a lot of questions about why we had a lot of groceries in our home. He asked why he and his brother didn't have any cereal at their house. Initially, we didn't think much of his line of questioning, but we made sure he was able to take some cereal home. As Marcus and Terry continued to visit us weekly, we began to receive more pieces to the puzzles. Marcus told his father that his mother was not feeding them. He also provided graphic details about being a witness to his mother being beaten up by her boyfriend, during which he once saw her boyfriend throw a microware on top of her while she was down on the floor. He further reported that his mother kept a lot of company all through the day and night. Deon took Marcus' allegations seriously, since his son was eight years old and certainly had no reason to make up false allegations against his mother.

We became very concerned about the boys. I encouraged Deon to take Rita to court for full custody of his sons. He filed a petition for full custody against Rita, and she was furious when she found out. Deon's attorney informed him that the process for seeking custody was lengthy and went over the initial steps with him. The first step was for the court to conduct a home study. This home study would provide the court a clear picture of what was best for the children. The court proceeded with the home studies for both Rita's and our home. After the home studies were completed, we waited to hear the court's findings.

Soon, Deon received an envelope from the court with the results. The court concluded that it was best for the children to remain in their home with Rita. We didn't understand how the court had made such an egregious error. Deon took the court's findings personal and felt like he had failed his children, but his hands were now tied.

Deon had some suspicions that Rita was indulging in drugs. It frustrated him that he couldn't get anyone in the community to confirm his suspicions. Rita's mother June was an enabler. She had aided her daughter in obtaining favorable results with her home study. Both Rita and June had rehearsed Marcus and Terry in their answers to the questions they were asked by the investigator. What they reported to the investigator was very different than the information Marcus had reported to his father, and June was in denial about her daughter's addiction.

After Deon failed to obtain full custody of his children, he vowed to wash his hands of the entire situation. I could tell that he was devastated. I had never seen him like that before. I tried to reassure him that in time everything would be all right, but Rita started taunting Deon. Every opportunity she got, she rubbed in his face the fact that she had been victorious in keeping their children. The situation began to greatly affect me, too, so I continued to seek the advice of my spiritual mentor, and she taught me how to pray about the situation when I was stressed out.

Rita began threatening to take him to court for more child support and made good on that threat when she hauled Deon into court. She was successful in getting her child support payments modified. The judge increased her weekly child support payments and included a clothing allowance. The amount of the clothing allowance was to be based on the amount of overtime Deon received each quarter. He was angry with the judge. He couldn't believe that his hard-earned money was going toward the purchase of drugs and wouldn't be used for his children who continued to go hungry at times. Deon continued to hear rumors from various people who lived in Rita's neighborhood that his children were roaming the streets in search of food.

Eight months after I started working at the plant, Deon received a call from the Child Protection Agency. They told him that they had received an anonymous telephone call regarding the neglect of his children and requested that he come to their office immediately. When we arrived, Deon was provided with the details of the alleged neglect of his children that had been filed against Rita. Someone in the community had finally decided to step up and do the right thing.

"Deon we need you to take temporary custody of your children," the caseworker reported.

"I've been waiting a long time to do that," he commented.

The caseworker stressed that Rita would still have the opportunity to get the children back, provided she adhered to the guidelines imposed upon her. The caseworker also called June in for questioning. After intense questioning, June admitted that she was aware that Rita was not taking proper care of her children. She also confirmed that her daughter used drugs. June further reported that she and her ex-husband often stood guard in front of Rita's house to chase off people who came to indulge in drugs with her. June begged the caseworker not to make the allegations of neglect against her daughter public. June wanted to protect her family's reputation as best she could. June gave Deon her blessing to temporarily take care of Marcus and Terry while her daughter received the help she needed. June was counting on Rita to clean up her act.

Deon and I made arrangements to pick up the children at the end of their school day. They were happy to see us. Marcus asked his father why we were picking them up, and Deon reassured them that everything was all right and told them that they would be living at our house for a while but would still be able to see their mother.

Marcus seemed relieved to hear the news, since he had been subjected to the majority of the distress while living with his mother. It was Marcus who had been forced to take care of Terry when his mother did not. He made sure they ate by taking his brother around their neighborhood to ask for food when they were hungry. When he was just two years old, his mother left them home alone. He was playing with matches and nearly burned down their apartment complex. Marcus had been through a lot of stress for a child. There were many red flags that had been missed which indicated that Rita was an unfit mother. Her children had needed to be removed from her care a lot earlier than they had been. It was understandable why the children were relieved to be going to a stable home.

We lived in a small three-bedroom house, and the expansion of our family caused us to consider increasing our living space. We made arrangements for Marcus and Terry to share a bedroom with my sons, Rasheed and Kashif who were around the same age. The transition was fairly easy for them since they had previously spent a significant amount of time around each other.

Things were going pretty good with Marcus and Terry living with us. Everyone was doing well in school and seemed happy, and Deon and I had the income necessary to provide for a family of seven.

A few months after the children moved into our home, my immediate supervisor approached me, "You're being transferred to the second shift," he reported.

"Do I have any other options?" I questioned.

He hadn't provided me with any advance warning, and the news was problematic. Deon and I didn't have time to find a reliable babysitter to help out with the children in the evenings. Besides our immediately babysitter issue, I wanted to be at home with my children to ensure that structure remained. It was imperative that I remain on the day shift, so I thought about ways to overrule my supervisor's decision, and a co-worker advised me that I qualified for a hardship transfer. Hardship transfers are given to employees who have extenuating circumstances, such as births, adoptions, divorce, and the like. I certainly had extenuating circumstances, so I submitted the paperwork necessary to apply for one. I was successful in getting transferred back to the day shift to take care of my family. My being on the day shift really made a difference with managing our household. Things just ran a lot smoother when I was at home. I have always been able to multi-task and enjoyed taking care of our children and my husband.

The problems with Rita continued, as she struggled to adhere to her court-ordered requirements to get her children back. Rita blamed us for her inadequacies and never took responsibility for her own actions. Deon never seemed to be affected by Rita's attacks and the backlash we received from the community in the same way I was. The entire situation was getting the best of me.

We continued to take care of our blended family. Deon had a soft spot for his children. I believe that the neglect they had received from their mother really bothered him a lot, but he didn't know how to deal with it. What he saw in his children resonated with him and his life as a child. It was a mirror image. I embraced the idea of supporting Deon with raising his children. In fact, it was my compassion for children that caused me to gravitate to them and become sensitive to their needs.

Once Rita realized that she wasn't going to get her children back, she went deeper into her addiction, and Deon was granted full custody of them. However, we would soon realize how naïve we were about how the effects of being neglected and abandoned can manifest in children. Deon and I didn't know that his children were masking emotional and behavioral issues. Nor did we consider the fact that they had many unidentified propensities. We did our best to make them feel comfortable and to address their individuals issues. One of the first things we noticed was that they lacked self-esteem. We worked hard to help Marcus and Terry feel better about themselves by encouraging them to be successful in every area of their life — especially in school. Marcus was already struggling in school. He had been previously held back a grade and was struggling to catch up. It was very challenging trying to bring him up to speed.

Prior to Marcus and Terry moving in with us, I had spent many years establishing structure and instilling the desire to be successful in my children. Rasheed, Anne, and Kashif were always successful in school and very well behaved. Deon and I walked a fine line to ensure our children weren't compared to one another or made to feel that there was any competition. Marcus and Terry weren't used to living in a structured environment. They found themselves inundated with structure and challenged with new expectations. Deon and I rewarded our children for getting good grades in school with praise and monetary incentives. The only stipulation we imposed on them was that they were expected to receive a letter grade above "D" or "F" in every subject. The monetary incentives and praise seemed to work fairly well for a while.

Rita made the transition from absent parent to a deserter. She walked away from her children and everything she knew to indulge in drugs. The children only saw her on rare occasions, since their mother officially chose drugs over them. She went on a hiatus that would last for years. That hiatus was good for us, but it proved to have some long-term effects on the children. We had no idea that their behaviors and attitudes stemmed for being abandoned. We would soon find out just how much.

It was September, 1995 when we began the construction of our brand-new house. It was a very exciting time for Deon and me. We needed the additional space for our large family. Being able to build a brand-new house was rewarding for us, and we were well on our way to living a comfortable lifestyle. We had a lot of control in the planning of the new house, and we decided to build a two-story house on the corner lot of our sub-division. We selected our floor plan: four bedrooms, two and half baths, dining room, living area, family room, kitchen, and a three-car garage.

Our moving into a new house meant that our children would be required to transfer to new schools, and they were all pretty excited about moving. We went shopping to pick out new furnishings for our new house and made plans to sell our current one. We enjoyed our last Christmas in our old house and anticipated the opportunities that the New Year would provide us.

It was January, 1996; the building of our new house was completed. There was no doubt that we were ready to move in. Most of our new neighbors welcomed us to the neighborhood. There were plenty of children in the neighborhood for our kids to play with. Most of the boys loved the fact that we had four boys, which made it easy for them to form instant sports teams or play various outdoor games. We purchased new bicycles for our children so they could easily explore our new neighborhood. Our children seemed to thrive in their new schools, and they loved our new house. The move was good for all of us. We encouraged our children to participate in sports and were lucky to have the Police Athletic League (PAL) program adjacent to our backyard. The PAL program sponsored various activities for the kids, such as football, soccer, cheerleading, and basketball, and it was really convenient for them to jump the fence to go to practice. I was heavily involved in the PAL programs and volunteered as a cheerleading coach for the cheerleading squads of the teams our sons played football on. It was truly a family sports venture.

A couple of years passed, and Rita continued to indulge in drugs. Her drug of choice was crack cocaine. She eventually became strung out on crack and was homeless. We would read the local newspaper to find out how she was doing. The Kokomo paper discloses arrest information weekly. It wasn't unusual for us to see Rita's name in the paper listed as one of the detainees. Deon and I became increasingly annoyed with Rita's lack of interest in seeking treatment for her addiction. We really didn't understand her addiction, and, as a result — we despised her.

June was very enabling and lax with Rita in her addiction and desperately aided her, hoping that she would one day get off drugs. We found June's laxness despicable when it came to Marcus and Terry. We were sensitive to the fact that she was heartbroken about her daughter's condition. However, she wasn't trustworthy when we allowed her to see her grandchildren in her daughter's absence. We firmly expressed our wishes and requested that she keep the children away from Rita. We wanted Rita to be responsible and to adhere to the court's orders, but we believed that June's permissiveness was causing Rita to be stagnating in her effort to achieve abstinence from drugs. June made things easy for Rita by sneaking behind our backs and allowing her to see her children whenever she had the opportunity. Despite this, we never penalized the children by not allowing them to see their grandmother. Deon knew it was important for them to have some family ties.

June didn't respect the fact that we had five children to care for and the challenges that went along with that responsibility. One thing that June did that I found frustrating was to show disparity between our children. However, her sister Marie was different. Marie supported Deon and me in every way. She deeply appreciated my helping to care for her great nephews in their mother's absence. Marie went out of her way to make our children feel loved and included. She always purchased comparable Christmas presents for them to their delight. She had a nice home with an outdoor swimming pool, and she invited them often to her home to swim. She loved to spoil them, to grill food for them, bring their favorite treats, and praise them for their hard work in school. She was a very important part of our plan for raising a successful blended family. All of our children loved Marie. Deon and I did as well.

On the other hand, June seemed to be tearing down the very foundation Deon and I had so carefully fashioned. She made a constant effort to compensate for her daughter's absences. In doing so, she often sidestepped our wishes. She loved to purchase a lot of Christmas presents for Marcus and Terry. On the surface, it seemed natural for a grandmother to spoil her own grandchildren, "That's what grandmothers do."

However, our issue with her was based on her opposition to our choice of raising all our children as equals. Our main priority was to raise them as brothers and sisters. In doing so, we made sure that all our children had an equal amount of Christmas presents, but June always over-compensated for Rita, which disrupted that equation. Our Christmas tradition was to open Christmas presents on Christmas Eve. As a family, we'd sit down in front of the Christmas tree, and all the children would take turns opening an equal amount of presents to their delight. However, on Christmas Day, Marcus and Terry visited their grandmother, and upon their return, they would enter our home with bags of additional Christmas presents. To add insult to injury, June would send my children one obviously less comparable present to open. June had no acceptance or sensitivity for our desire to merge our blended family with love and inclusion.

I grew frustrated and often felt offended by her actions. I had taken good care of June's grandchildren in her daughter's absence over the years, and I wasn't going to allow anyone to treat my children badly, whether knowingly or unknowingly. June was showing disparity between our children. She was sending the wrong message to her grandchildren, too. Our children all had similar losses. My children lost their father when he was killed, while her grandchildren lost their mother to the streets. As far as I was concerned, they were all on an equal playing field, and they all needed love and sensitivity.

The one thing that our five children had in common was Deon's and my willingness to come together to provide them with two loving parents and a middle-class lifestyle. I couldn't understand June's inability to comprehend our unique situation the same way her sister Marie did. Showing disparity in blended families eventually causes a rift. It would have been appropriate for her to provide her grandchildren whatever she desired, if they were living with their mother. I guess I was naïve to believe that other people shared my same mindset when it came to raising children. I believe there has to be a certain level of sensitivity for children's feelings when they are raised in blended families, especially if the root cause is from death or abandonment. I explained to Deon how June's actions bothered me. I pleaded with him to talk to her about the situation, but he didn't seem to want to take up the issue with her. I was surprised that he wouldn't back me up the way I needed him to.

He never said a word to her about the situation, and I became even more frustrated that my feelings were being ignored by my own husband, so I decided to talk to Marie about the situation. She provided me with a sympathetic ear and suggested that I divide the presents equally between our children once Marcus and Terry returned home from their grandmother's house on Christmas Day. Marie's suggestion sounded good in theory, but it wasn't a realistic option. I wasn't going to take Christmas presents from Marcus and Terry that they had opened on Christmas Day at their grandmother's house. My spiritual mentor did her best to encourage me and always asked me to pray about the situation.

Once I realized that I wasn't going to receive any support from Deon, I decided to take matters into my own hands, and I made allowances for the disparity that June was showing my children. I decided to reduce the amount of Christmas presents we purchased for Marcus and Terry knowing that they would receive additional presents on Christmas Day from their grandmother. I purchased additional Christmas presents for Rasheed, Anne, and Kashif to make up for the disparity. I felt it was the best resolution. It was apparent that Rita and some members of her family's actions were impacting the success of our blended family. I thought it was sad that adults couldn't work together for the best interest of all our children. Incidents such as these helped to aid the many challenges I would later face.

CHAPTER 27

Acceptance: Raising Children Can Be Hard

Deon and I have very different parenting styles, and our children were savvy enough to know the differences. Marcus and Terry perceived me as being the strict parent who pushed for discipline and structure. Their assumptions were correct! I believe wholeheartedly in addressing behavioral issues at the onset.

Deon, on the other hand, is passive about everything and doesn't say much. He generally lets things build up and then he explodes. For the most part, he left the handing out of punishments up to me. One of the reasons was that his busy work schedule dictated his absence from home. The other reason was simply avoidance. However, I always talked to him about the consequences that I deemed appropriate in each situation, and Deon was always in agreement with me about the way situations were handled. However, he never verbally re-emphasized the reasons for those decisions to his children, nor did he vocally back me up, and this always made me look like the "bad guy" to them since his children generally received the majority of the discipline. There were times when I would delay issuing discipline to them to allow Deon to handle things. I would often regret handling things that way because he would either be too tired to address issues or would simply forget, thus leaving situations to go unaddressed. When that happened, it fueled my frustration and further led to their assumption that I was out to get them.

I believe the main reason why Deon was so passive about disciplining Marcus and Terry was because he didn't know how to deal with their reoccurring behaviors. His children were a constant reminder of his childhood. Growing up, Deon did not have anyone to correct his behavior since he had also been abandon by his mother. He had been left alone to raise himself from the age of sixteen to adulthood. As a result of his abandonment, he became a troubled youth. Deon's father had also disappointed him. His father never came to any of his sporting activities although Deon was an outstanding athlete. With the proper guidance, Deon could have easily played baseball or football in college or professionally. Deon's father lived a comfortable life on the other side of town with his wife and son. He never took an active role in his son's life.

When Deon and I first moved to Kokomo, I encourage him to mend his broken relationship with his estranged father, and they were able to find some common ground through forgiveness. Deon didn't have an example of what good parenting skills looked like. It seemed that the only person who cared about his success was his grandfather who made an immense impact on his life. When his grandfather died, Deon was left to feel alone.

Deon and I were both sensitive to Marcus and Terry's abandonment issues. We did a good job of be respectful whenever we talked about their mother to them. The majority of our conversation regarding their mother always had one consistent message. We ensured them that when their mother made the choice to adhere to her court-ordered plan, then they would be able to see her. Deon and I had an ax to grind with Rita for not financially supporting her children. After Deon received full custody of Marcus and Terry, she racked up thousands of dollars in back child support. The court never supported him in making her accountable to the same standards that had been imposed on him when he was ordered to pay her child support. Instead, Rita was given a free pass since she had an addiction.

Deon and I anticipated that the day would come when Rita would be legally able to have visitation with her sons. Marcus exhibited a lot more behavioral issues than Terry, and we were constantly receiving telephone calls from the school regarding his behavior. His grades were declining, so we spent a lot of time talking to him and attempting to help him identify the root causes for his poor behavior. We also wanted to make sure that he had a clear understanding of what was expected of him. After continuous failed attempts to get him to change his behavior and comply with our rules, he left us with no other option but to discipline him. He was often grounded to his room. We also sought therapy for him. Marcus attended a few sessions, but we decided to remove him from therapy after we learned that one of his group members was providing the entire group with accounts of Rita's street life, details which a child should never have to hear about his mother from a stranger. Deon and I were unsuccessful at getting Marcus' attention. It seemed that he had no desire to improve no matter how many consequences resulted. It was apparent that we weren't the individuals to reach Marcus. His propensities had a strong hold on him and wouldn't let go.

Deon and I had to be consistent with our expectations for all our children, since there was simply too much at stake. Terry was different from Marcus in that he had a lot of pride. He really cared what people thought about him. He wanted to excel in school, and he worked hard to stay out of trouble. It seemed to really bother him that his mother was homeless and strung-out on drugs. There were a couple of occasions when Terry and I ran into his mother Rita while we were out shopping. She was barely recognizable as a result of her drug use, and Terry seemed to be so embarrassed each time he saw her. I could always tell by the look on his face that it hurt him to see his mother that way. Seeing Rita in that condition was also awkward for me. We never knew what to say to each other, so we never said anything at all.

Deon and I did the best we could with raising our five children while working full-time jobs. Deon took on the role as the provider for our family. He loved spending money and buying nice things. Deon hardly ever misses work, and it isn't unusual for him to work twelve hours a day, seven days a week — when the work is available. Deon is the workhorse of the family, and I am the caretaker. We both take our roles seriously. I had no problem taking care of the shopping, budgeting, taking the children to practices, cleaning, cooking, working fulltime, and being a wife. We got along pretty well despite a few bumps in the road that came from Deon's past baggage and the challenges associated with raising a blended family.

CHAPTER 28

Acceptance: Following The Voice of God

It was 1997; Deon and I learned though a mutual friend that Rita was pregnant. Initially, I was in disbelief since she was strung-out on drugs. My first thought was that Rita didn't need to have any more children, especially since she wasn't taking care of the two she already had. Marcus and Terry were very happy when they found out that their mother was pregnant, despite her absence in their lives. I think they believed that her pregnancy was a positive sign that she was in recovery. It wasn't long after Rita's baby was delivered that the Child Protection Agency stepped in and removed her baby from her care. They were able to substantiate the removal based on her continuous drug use. At just four months old, Rita's daughter was placed in foster care.

No one in Rita's immediately family volunteered to be a relative for the placement of her daughter. The family court intervened, and, consequently, Rita's daughter became a statistic of the foster care system. Her daughter was found to be a Child In Need of Services (CHINS). When I heard about Rita's daughter being in foster care,

143

I taken aback. I couldn't believe that her family had allowed that to happen. I decided to contact the Child Protection Agency to inquire about her daughter.

"Is it possible for Marcus and Terry to visit their sister in her current foster care placement?" I asked the caseworker.

"I have to ask Rita," she reported.

After waiting for a few days to hear her decision, the caseworker informed me that Rita had denied my request. I was appalled. I couldn't believe that Rita would deny her own children the right to visit their sister, especially since she wasn't taking care of her. I politely thanked the caseworker and realized that I had done all I could. Deon and I went on with our lives, raising our five children. We decided to enroll in college to pursue getting an Associate's Degree in Business Management. Going to college meant that I needed to make sure our household was organized and had a lot of structure. It was the only way we would be successful in college. We enrolled and were scheduled to attended classes one night a week. Deon's brother David offered to babysit our children, which was really a blessing.

It wasn't long after we started college that we learned about Deon's mother being gravely ill, and he took on additional responsibilities to assist his grandmother with the care of his mother. He loved his mother, even though she hadn't been there for him during some periods of his childhood. His mother continued to get worse. I supported him throughout his mother's illness, and I was sensitive to the pain he endured while watching her health deteriorate. Deon visited his mother daily to massage her pain-stricken body. She died right before his eyes, and he was devastated. The night prior to his mother's death, she made peace with me while lying in her hospital bed.

"I need you to take care of my mother and to continue to make my son happy," she said.

"You've got my word," I replied.

I adored Deon's grandmother and was more than happy to honor his mother's final wishes. In fact, I was happy that she had asked me to help.

When Rita's daughter was about eleven months old, I received a call from the caseworker who I had spoken to some months earlier. She informed me that Rita was doing a lot better and explained that the court was considering giving her a second chance to care for her daughter.

"Are you and your family still interested in visiting with the baby?" she asked.

"Why do you ask?" I inquired.

"I need to establish a plan B," she said.

The caseworker told me that the baby's foster mother was very upset about the court findings. The baby's foster mother didn't think it was fair to remove the baby from her care since she had taken care of her for eleven months, and she vowed not to take Rita's baby back into her home if things didn't work out with the real mother.

Rita was given back her baby daughter, and they moved into June's house. The court wanted to make sure Rita had a place to stay, and June was deemed responsible to oversee things. On a couple of occasions, Deon allowed Marcus and Terry to visit their grandmother while Rita was living there. He wanted them to have the opportunity to spend some time with their sister. After one of the visits, I went over to June's house to pick them up. June greeted me at my car with the children. I noticed Rita standing on the porch with her daughter in her arms.

"May I hold the baby?" I asked.

June looked to Rita for permission and she agreed. I held the baby in my arms, and she seemed happy as she stared deeply into my eyes. We made an instant connection that would later change her life. I asked June if it was possible for Rita's daughter to come to our house occasionally to spend some quality time with Marcus and Terry. June said that she would have to discuss it with Rita, but I wasn't surprised that she didn't really take my request seriously, but while driving home, I had a strange premonition. God spoke to my spirit and provided me with specific details of His will for Rita's daughter's life.

"You will raise Rita's daughter," was the audible message I received.

"It will not be easy; however, it is your assignment," was the second half of the message.

I hurried into the house to share my premonition with Deon. He found my revelation to be farfetched and reminded me that we already had our hands full with raising our own five children. Deon said that he had no desire to raise Rita's child who wasn't even his. I also dismissed the thought, and we went on with our lives.

In July of 1998, Deon and I received a telephone call from Marie, "Rita has run off again and has abandoned her daughter," Marie explained.

"Oh, my God," I said. "Where is she?" I asked.

"My daughter is caring for her, but she has to go to work," she told me.

Rita had left her baby at Marie's daughter's house for a couple of days, and they had some serious concerns about the baby's welfare. Rita's mother June had gone out of town for a few days, leaving Rita home alone in the house to care for her daughter. With no one around to hold her accountable, she had made the choice to leave her daughter alone so she could go do drugs. I told Marie that we had once considered taking care of the child and asked Marie for her permission to contact the caseworker at the Child Protection Agency to report the incident.

"My wishes are to keep the baby in the family. I want either Rita's sister or you all to take care of her," Marie said.

I contacted the caseworker and reported the information, "We want to be the caretakers," I asserted.

"That's great, but the court would prefer a relative placement," she explained.

However, Rita's sister wavered when asked directly to care for her niece. She had concerns about not being financially able to, since she was a single parent. The caseworker was obligated to inform the court about Rita's sister's concerns. The Family Court judge was now forced to take action to make a permanency plan for Rita's daughter. After giving consideration to the facts, the judge rendered her decision. She decided to place Rita's daughter in our care. Her decision was based on the fact that we were already the caretakers of Rita's two other children. The judge rendered that it would be best for all three of Rita's children to be together. At that moment, Deon realized that my premonition was spot on! It was God's will for Rita's daughter to be with us. Deon and I embraced God's will with open arms, but we had no idea that by following God's will we would face a lot of unpleasant trials and tribulations.

When the judge's decision reached Rita's family, all hell broke loose. They were furious and embarrassed. While the judge was deliberating her decision, Rita's daughter had been temporarily placed in Rita's mother's home. Rita's family had believed that the judge would rule in their favor, so they made some plans for Rita's daughter to live with her sister for a while in Indianapolis. The caseworker asked if we had an issue with going to Indianapolis to pick up Rita's daughter from her sister's house. We were excited and didn't mind making the hour-long trip there. The caseworker also assured us that the transferring of Rita's daughter would be smooth and there would be no need for police intervention. However, the caseworker was unaware that Rita was staying with her sister in Indianapolis. Her sister was allowing her to stay there to assist her with the care of her daughter.

Deon and I packed up our five children and headed to Indianapolis. Marcus and Terry were especially excited about their sister coming to live with us. When we arrived at Rita's sister's apartment complex, Deon called to let her know we were there. She brought Rita's daughter out to our car.

"Why are you doing this?" she asked.

"Please give us the baby," Deon pleaded.

She asked the same question several times while attempting to prolong transferring Rita's daughter. She finally handed her niece to me without incident, and Rita never came outside of her sister's apartment. We headed back to Kokomo with Rita's daughter, Mia.

Mia was a happy baby, and she warmed up to us quickly. I could tell that she was at peace. I attempted to learn all I could about her from her foster mother. Mia's foster mother was more than happy to provide me with specific details about her. She indicated that Mia had a few allergies and always kept a cold. She also warned me that it was possible I would have to miss a lot of work, as she did frequently, to care for Mia. I learned that Mia was a carrier of the Sickle Cell Anemia trait. Deon and I wondered what other challenges she would bring besides the fact that she was still in diapers. We made arrangements for her to share a room with my daughter Anne, who was more than eager to help out. For years, Anne had been the only girl, but she welcomed the presence of another girl in the house.

Our problems with Rita intensified once Mia moved into our home. She began to spread rumors about Deon and me. Rita needed to justify why her daughter had been removed from her care and feared that Deon and I would expose her dirty little secret. Some of the rumors Rita spread were ridiculous. The most outlandish one we heard from some of our associates in the community was that we had stolen her daughter from her family. Even though most people knew otherwise, some wanted to believe the rumors anyway. Another vicious lie she told was that Deon was a drug dealer and I practiced witchcraft. Some members of the community thought we were callous and cold for stepping up to care for Rita's daughter.

It seemed that most people were really naive when it came to understanding how the Family Court system worked. Typically, mothers are always given an opportunity to comply with the court's wishes before their children are taken from them. Their reunification with their children takes preference above all else unless circumstances warrant otherwise. Rita and her family were able to cover up the fact that Mia had been a ward of the state since the age of four months. They were able to easily manipulate Mia's White foster mother. She felt sorry for Rita and allowed her family a lot of flexibility with visitations outside the scope of the court order.

Rita didn't waste any time in her attempt to have Mia removed from our care. Right away, she informed the caseworker that she didn't want her daughter to be placed in our home. Rita cited the fact that we were not blood relatives of her daughter and demanded that she be removed.

The caseworker called us, "I just want to warn you guys that the judge may remove Mia from your care," she informed me.

"Why?" I questioned.

"You and Deon are not blood relatives," she replied.

149

We quickly addressed her complaint by completing the paperwork necessary to become Mia's legal foster parents. Once we obtained our foster parent license, there wasn't anything Rita could do. Her objections were put to rest! The only option she had was to get clean and take responsibility for her own actions. June's codependency kicked in again when she hired a private attorney to represent her in obtaining grandparent visitations. June wanted to save face for the family. She was convinced that we were personally attacking her family by volunteering to take care of her granddaughter. June petitioned the court for grandparent visitations and was granted supervised visitations with Mia once a week. The sad part about June's actions was that the court originally wanted her to volunteer to become a relative placement for Mia. The court encouraged her to convince Rita to allow her to have guardianship of Mia. If those measures had been taken, she could have saved a lot of time, money, and embarrassment.

As Mia's foster parents, Deon and I were required to transport Mia to specific locations for the court-ordered visitations with relatives. Shortly after June was granted visitations with Mia, Rita was too. She cleaned up well enough to be granted supervised visitations. Being Mia's foster parents also meant that we had to deal with all of Rita's dysfunction and family dynamics. It proved to be very stressful. We were privy to all her personal information regarding her addiction. We went through some of the highs and lows that plagued her, as she tried to put her life back together. Rita manipulated the court system as much as she could in her attempts to get Mia back. There were so many times when Deon and I wanted to throw in the towel. We got so tired of the crap! God gave us a tough assignment, but He also provided us with the endurance to see things through to their completion.

Rita failed to remain drug free and wouldn't comply with her court-ordered plan. The court was forced to intervene and revoked her visitations with Mia. June petitioned the court to have her supervised visitations modified and requested to have unsupervised visits with Mia in her home. June did everything she could to make things easy for her daughter to see Mia just as she had done with Marcus and Terry. The court was very responsive to all of June's requests, and Deon and I never knew what to expect while we were Mia's foster parents. It was like getting on a roller coaster at the amusement park and the operator refusing to let you off.

After Mia was in the court system for nearly twenty-four months as a Child in Need of Services (CHINS), the court recommended that the parental rights of both Rita and Mia's biological father Jack be terminated. When Deon and I learned that the court was finally going to seek the termination of parental rights against Rita and Jack, we were ecstatic. We were now free to legally adopt Mia. Our family had become very attached to Mia during her yearlong placement in our home.

It was 2000; things were going pretty good for Deon and me. We had recently completed our Associates Degree and were pretty proud of that accomplishment, and we were getting closer to our dreams of advancement at the plant.

We learned that Deon's grandmother had a stroke that was followed by a few mini-strokes. Her doctor prescribed some medications to slow down the process. Deon kept a watchful eye over his *"Granny"*. We made frequent visits to the hospital and made sure that we understood how to properly care for her. However, her health continued to deteriorate and she died shortly thereafter. Deon and I believed she died from a broken heart from the loss of her daughter a few years earlier. Deon took her death very hard. He adored his grandmother and would do anything for her.

Later that year, Deon and I discussed having a formal wedding. I really wanted to have a traditional wedding, and I was very happy to finally be able to experience one. Both of my previous marriages had the same uneventful and rushed civil ceremonies. With Deon's blessing, I planned a small, traditional wedding for us with all the special touches.

"How much can I spend?" I asked.

"Whatever it takes to make you happy," Deon told me.

Our wedding party consisted of all our children, some family members, and a few friends. My wedding dress was breathtaking.

"You make a beautiful bride," Deon said.

Our wedding colors were black and gold, and all of the bridesmaids wore black and gold dresses. They all looked elegant. It was nice to have all our children participate in our vow renewal. Deon's father gave me away, which meant a lot to me. Mia was our flower girl. She wore a miniature wedding dress that closely resembled mine, and she was my little twin that day. Deon was very happy to give me the wedding I deserved.

A few months after we renewed our vows, our adoption of Mia was finalized, and Rita unsuccessfully appealed the court's decision. Mia was our daughter legally, so we decided to change her name. We changed it to Leah. She was issued a brand-new birth certificate which showed Deon and me as her parents. Leah's name change was ceremonious and represented her new journey and new life outside the court system. We were now officially responsible for the well-being of six children and continued to do our best to ensure that our children were provided with a loving home.

Once things settled down, Deon and I went back to school to pursue Bachelor's Degrees in Business Management. We wanted to take full advantage of the educational benefits that our employer offered. We also considered our long-term plans of advancing our careers within the plant. Both of us had a full plate that consisted of being parents, working fulltime jobs, providing our children with a good example by working hard, and we pursued a secondary education simultaneously. We wanted to make sure that we lived by our own example.

It was 2002; Deon and I received our Bachelor's Degrees from Indiana Wesleyan University. To finally graduate with a Bachelor's Degree was a crowning achievement for me. I had gone to college right after high school but had soon dropped out to work fulltime. After completing our Bachelor's Degrees, Deon received an opportunity to advance his career. He was invited to interview for a position in management as a supervisor. This was certainly one of the happiest I had ever seen him. We were both underdogs and had to fight hard to accomplish our goals. Deon passed his interview with flying colors and became a supervisor. It was certainly a defining moment for him. The news of Deon's promotion traveled quickly around town. He couldn't believe how many people were jealous of his success. As a teenager, he'd often been regarded as a hoodlum who was going nowhere fast, but he had proven everyone wrong by working hard and following his dreams. I was very proud of him.

The jealously came from all different directions, mostly family, but there were friends, too, who believed that they should benefit from his good fortune. Deon and I continued to enjoy our middle-class lives that we made for ourselves. We could afford the finer things in life, which included the purchase of many luxury cars and vacations. Deon added fast motorcycles to his list of toys. He loved to ride motorcycles and eventually started his own motorcycle club. Deon was earning the respect and adoration from some of his peers and worked a lot of hours in the plant. While he worked, I handled the majority of our household responsibilities.

It was 2003; I was relentless in my quest for career advancement at the plant, too. I made an effort to secure a position that would match my qualifications and searched for administrative positions. To increase my chances, I attempted to network with some individuals who worked in the front office. Once I realized that those leads weren't going to materialize, I decided to seek a position as a supervisor. I did a lot of legwork and positioned myself for the right opportunity. To my surprise, it didn't take long for me to be offered a supervisory position, and I was more than happy to accept the offer. For the first time in my life, I secured a white-collar job and was making a lot of money. I was very grateful for the opportunity. Living in Kokomo became a little more tolerable once I received my promotion.

CHAPTER 29

Acceptance: A Mother's Return

Of course, Deon and I still could not escape the wrath of Rita. Deon received notification that she was taking him to court for visitations with Marcus and Terry. We didn't view her return into their lives as a positive occurrence; however, we knew that the day would eventually come when she would be a part of their lives again. Marcus was now fifteen and Terry was thirteen.

Rita returned after being absent for nearly seven years. We imagined the drama that would ensue after their honeymoon period from the reunification wore off. Deon and I had some immediate concerns about her abstinence from drugs, although she was on her way to recovery. However, Rita still exhibited some of her old behaviors that we had disliked prior to her becoming addicted.

The court granted her supervised visitation and ordered her church mentor to supervise those visits. Rita began to rub it in Deon's face that she had regained visitations for their children. The court granted her permission to come to our house and knock on our front door once a week to pick up them. The judge also required Deon to provide her with our home telephone number. Rita abused her calling privileges right away. It wasn't uncommon to have multiple messages on our answering machine from Rita, especially when she felt like she was being ignored. After listening to a couple of them, we did ignore her. Most of the messages were continuous rants that were off subject and had very little to do with the children. Rita's presence was beginning to become irritating. It was stressful having my personal space invaded. She didn't seem to respect boundaries, and just hearing her voice on our answering machine made my skin crawl. The stressful environment that she was creating started to magnify once Leah became part of the equation.

Rita refused to let Deon and I forget that she was the birth mother of Leah. She would stoop to any level to see her and came pretty close to being a stalker. To get a glimpse of Leah, she would survey our neighborhood on days which she legally had permission to pick up her children. We didn't have any control over her picking up Marcus and Terry at our residence, but we did have the right to keep her from interacting with Leah. We made it clear to her that she was to have nothing to do with Leah, but Rita ignored our request several times.

We stayed on "HIGH ALERT" on the days she had permission to come to our house. There were a couple of occasions when she got lucky and did see Leah playing outside. She refused to show us respect and to accept our wishes. Once Rita established a comfortable relationship with Marcus and Terry, she began using them to try to make contact with Leah behind our back. Rita didn't waste any time attempting to bond with her children and to make up for the several years she had lost touch with them. She used a tactical approach to build her relationship with them. One of those tactics was to interrogate them for information.

"What do they do over there?" she'd ask.

She drilled them about everything regarding their happiness at our house instead of using that time to get to know them. She used their information as a launching pad for gaining control over them and went behind Deon's back by going to the children's respective schools to see them when she didn't have court-ordered visits. Slowly but surely, Rita began to manipulate them, and I must say it was working. Marcus and Terry were being pulled in different directions. The more they visited their mother, the more defiant they became when they returned home. They were receiving conflicting viewpoints and expectations from both parents. In Rita's attempt to make contact with Leah, she went as far as having one of Marcus' girlfriends who worked at Leah's school as a student aid to take a picture of her. The young girl told Leah that she took the picture of her for her "real mom". We were furious once we found out. I went to Leah's school and confronted the principal.

"You failed to protect our daughter's rights," I accused.

"I'm very sorry — I was unaware of the specifics," he pleaded.

"I expected you to discipline the young lady and to protect our rights," I demanded.

The principal had no knowledge of the entire scheme but fired the young girl immediately. He also advised me that a liaison police office had talked to Leah. The school received a call from The Child Protection Agency for a complaint that Leah was afraid in her own home. Deon and I concluded that Rita had made the anonymous call, although we didn't have any concrete evidence to support our suspicions. There was no end to her desperation. There were numerous times when I wanted to physically attack her for the hell she was putting us through, but I always remained the bigger person in order to provide our children with a good example.

Prior to Rita's return, Terry was doing well in school and his behavioral issues were minimal. However, once she returned, we noticed that he was displaying a lot of hidden anger and rebellion, especially after returning from her house. She looked in every direction but her own to find blame for her children's behavior issues. Their behavior was very different when they were at her house. She was still in the process of getting to know them and was using the parent/friend approach to parent them without success.

Rita and Marcus were getting into a lot of explosive arguments that would often result in him walking off from her. Deon vowed that he wouldn't get involved with correcting his children when he learned their behavior was less than acceptable while visiting their mother. He thought Rita needed to establish her own relationship with them, and he refused to co-parent with her. When they visited their mother, both Marcus and Terry were exhibiting behaviors that would never be tolerated in our house. Their behavior and the root cause for it continued to be the "big white elephant in the room" that no one talked about.

Terry started picking up some of Marcus' behaviors. One day, he decided to try out his newly-learned outburst on me as I attempted to discipline him. Needless to say, I wasn't pleased. As time passed, it seemed that Deon was scaling back on the way he dealt with them, too. It felt like we were fighting a losing battle. All the structure that we had once established was slowly dissipating, while Marcus and Terry were enjoying the benefit of transitioning between both households. They were dealing with two completely different sets of rules, and they were learning to manipulate others as well.

It was 2004; my son Rasheed was graduating from high school with honors. It was certainly a defining moment in both our lives. Rasheed received multiple letters of interest to attend some of the most prestigious colleges around the country. I was so proud of him. He decided to attend Purdue University on a full-ride tuition scholarship.

We moved Rasheed into his college dormitory, and he seemed to thrive on being away from home.

With Rasheed gone to college, Deon and I depended on the twins, Kashif and Anne, a lot more to help run the household after I learned that I had to return to the second shift at the plant. However, there wasn't anything I could do about the transfer this time. I was a member of management, which meant that I was required to be flexible and able to change shifts at a moment's notice. Kashif and Anne were very mature for their ages. They both had a driver's license and were able to assist with picking up and dropping off our children as needed.

Kashif was available to help out more than Anne, since she was a high school cheerleader and kept a busy schedule. I had no idea that Kashif was harboring some resentment against Deon and me for making him feel like a miniature parent in our absence. Kashif was very passive and often felt like he was being taken advantage of and placed in the middle of difficult situations.

We needed their help and could trust them to make sure things ran smoothly while we were at work. Unfortunately, we didn't have many of options. Our children were all old enough to be left home alone, and Deon's brother, David, pitched in to help out whenever he could and always made himself available for emergencies.

It was the summer of 2004; Deon and I learned that Rita was getting married. We hoped that she would finally get a life and focus on her new husband. I also hoped that she would have the opportunity to see what it was like to be on the other side of the coin. Her husband had children from previous relationships. I wanted her to see firsthand how difficult it was to manage blended families. Stepmothers don't typically get a lot of credit. I often felt like I was married to both Deon and Rita. It was good that she had someone else to focus her time and attention on.

It was 2005; Marcus continued to get into trouble. It seemed like even Rita's influence wasn't enough to help turn things around for him. Deon and I received a troubling telephone call from the high school that led to Marcus' permanent expulsion. After Marcus was permanently expelled from the local high school, he didn't have a lot of options. He still had yet another year of high school to complete, so I went around to some of the county schools to see if they would allow me to enroll him. I received a resounding "NO" with each request. I sat down to talk to him about his options.

"What do you really want to do with your life?" I asked.

"I want to get my GED — and join the army," he announced.

Deon and I helped Marcus enroll in a GED program. He studied hard and was able to pass the test. With a GED in hand, he was ready to speak with an army recruiter. Marcus had always wanted to follow in his father's footsteps and become a soldier, but Deon was skeptical about his son going into the Army National Guard. He had some concerns about the possibility of Marcus being shipped off to war. I encouraged Marcus to do what he wanted to do for a change. The idea of joining the Army National Guard seemed to motivate him. I believed that the Army National Guard was a positive move for Marcus; it would certainly provide him with the structure he desperately needed.

The size of our family was diminishing quickly when Marcus joined the National Guard and went off to basic training. We were proud of him, and we could see that he had an opportunity for new beginnings. Deon was happy that Marcus was following in his footsteps, and now, with Rasheed and Marcus away from the nest, we only had four children in our care.

I'd always had a love for God. I'd always maintained a personal relationship with Him throughout my life and was baptized when I was nine years old. Nevertheless, I continued to fight my demons: *fear, depression, and isolation.* Living in Kokomo and dealing with all the challenges that came along with Deon's baggage brought my demons to the forefront of my mind. I felt trapped and addicted to dysfunction. I found it difficult to break free from my misery, so I began using food as a coping mechanism to escape my pain, but I realized that I had a family to take care of and that I didn't have the option of being weak, so I decided to join a local church. I needed an outlet for dealing with all the stress I was encountering, while suffering in silence from all the trials and tribulations. Deon never seemed to understand how I could allow other people's personal attacks to tear me down. He always acted like things didn't bother him, although they did.

"Why do you allow these damn people to get on your nerves?" he asked often.

Our differences in the way we processed the attacks made it hard for me to get the sympathy I needed from him. I dealt with my addiction to dysfunction by becoming a comfort-food addict. Attending church seemed to be a good decision, since every time I attend, I begin to feel stronger. The pastor always seems to have a right-now word for me with each sermon I listen to. I love the church I attend. It feels good to have a church home full of parishioners to cover me in prayer.

I soon made every attempt to free myself from my old ways of coping with things, and I began to feel better mentally, emotionally, and spiritually.

However, I developed a health issue that needed my attention. I started having a lot of problems with my menstrual cycle. Over the years, I began losing more and more blood during my menstrual cycles. I was also experiencing a lot of clotting. I went to see my doctor for a consultation. He explained the reasons why individuals have heavy menstrual cycles and recommended that I have a Hysterectomy. I researched my options and decided to have the procedure. During the procedure, I lost a lot of blood and had to have a blood transfusion. I was upset when I learned that I needed a blood transfusion. However, I agreed to have it because I knew it was necessary.

After the procedure, I believed that I would experience a normal recovery. However, I began to have a lot of complications. The nurses weren't providing me with adequate care, which forced me to ring the nurse's bell several times a day just to get the attention I needed. There were a couple of occasions when my dripback ran completely dry. After being hospitalized for a few days, my doctor told me that I had an infection, and my infection was causing me to have a high fever, but the doctors couldn't seem to identify the root cause for my elevated temperature. The staff administered a significant amount of tests, but to no avail. My doctor told me that I couldn't be released from the hospital until my high fever dissipated.

I felt so alone, although Deon visited me daily and returned home in the evenings with the children. I told him that I was very disturbed by the substandard care I was receiving from the nurses. Deon was ready to confront the nurses, but I asked him not to. I began to feel like I was admitted to the hospital and trapped there to die.

I told Deon that I was going to call my pastor and ask him to pray for my release from the hospital. I declared that I was going to pray my way out, so I called my pastor and left a message on the hotline. I really didn't expect him to call me back that same day, since it was Sunday. The church I attend has a very large congregation, so I expected someone other than the pastor to return my call — like a member of his staff. To my surprise, my pastor called me back that afternoon.

"What can I help you with?" he asked.

"Pastor, I need prayer. I've been in the hospital for days, and they can't find what's wrong with me," I reported.

He began to pray with me. My high fever dissipated that evening, and I was released from the hospital the very next morning. I was thankful that God hears the prayers of His people.

My doctor advised me that I should expect to gain some weight after having my Hysterectomy. Subsequently, I gained about twenty pounds right away — to my disappointment.

It was 2006; Anne and Kashif were graduating from high school. They were also college bound. I couldn't have been more proud of them. It brought me great solace to know that my three children had beaten the odds and were seeking a post-secondary education. I wished that their father was alive to enjoy their success. Anne was accepted into Indiana University, and Kashif was accepted into Ball State University. With the twins heading off to college, we were down to only two children at home.

Rita continued to pick up Terry for visits. One evening, I had to work overtime and left Terry home alone with Leah. Terry was sixteen years old, so there was no concern. Rita was scheduled to pick him up later that evening. I realized that there would be at least a thirty-minute gap between the time Rita was scheduled to him up and the time I arrived home. Knowing that I had advised Terry and Leah to stay in their rooms and watch television, I felt reasonably comfortable that they would do what I requested of them.

Over the years, Deon and I had to limit the amount of access Marcus and Terry had to Leah. Rita used them to violate our trust by asking them to tell Leah certain things about herself. Leah had no idea that she was adopted. We wanted to wait until she was a teen to tell her, but Marcus and Terry would hint around about certain thing when talking to her. We could never trust them around her. I didn't think Leah would come out of her room to interact with Terry in my absence. However, I was wrong. When Rita arrived to pick Terry up, he lured Leah out of her room by asking her to come downstairs to help him carry his bags outside. Terry was fully aware that we didn't allow his mother to have any contact with Leah, but Leah innocently agreed to help Terry. When Leah went outside, she found Terry's mother outside waiting there to talk to her. Rita capitalized on the opportunity to talk to Leah.

"I'm your real mom," she told Leah.

She gave her a hug and sent her back inside the house. Rita was annoyed that Leah would be left home alone after she left with Terry. Once they arrived at their destination, she advised Terry to call home and leave a message for me on our answering machine. When I returned home, I noticed that Terry was gone and I checked our messages. Terry had left a scripted message. Leah told me about the drama of the evening, and she was devastated to learn from Rita that she was adopted. It was bad enough that Rita was so inconsiderate, but I couldn't believe that Terry had participated in her scheme. I called Deon right away, and he was furious, too.

Up to that point, Leah had no idea she was adopted. As Leah's adoptive parents, it was up to us to decide when and how we wanted to tell our daughter about her previous life. Deon and I couldn't wrap our minds around his children's loyalty to Rita. We had taken good care of them during her seven years hiatus, and we understood that they yearned for a relationship with her, but Terry had no right to interfere with our desires as Leah's parents. It was our worst nightmare. Rita's selfishness had reached a new low. It was a shame that she would pit her own children against their father and me, and it was very hard to find acceptance for all of this.

Rita fueled what was becoming a strained relationship between Terry and me. As our relationship deteriorated, I began to pull back on my attempts to parent him. I simply allowed Deon to address our joint concerns, and I began to keep quiet about my feelings regarding the behavior of Marcus and Terry. Deon didn't address a lot of things that were going on with Terry and his behavior, so I began to become frustrated. Terry seemed to enjoy the fact that he was having his way at both our houses, and the situation began to put a strain on Deon's and my relationship. Terry became the "big elephant" in the room that no one wanted to address. I felt like I couldn't say anything about Terry. Rita influence was destroying my marriage, and there were times when I didn't even want come home. I was becoming so bitter on the inside.

CHAPTER 30

Disappointment: Farewell to a Father

It was 2007; I received word from a distant cousin that my father was gravely ill. A few years prior to learning of his illness, I had tried to reach out to him and was successful in locating him. When we finally had the opportunity to talk, I learned that he'd never remarried. My father had a long-term girlfriend who was his life partner. "Hey, Daddy, I have a question," I announced.

"What's that?" he asked.

"Do I have any other siblings?" I wondered.

"No — just your sister," he told me.

After nearly forty years, my father was still in the Disappointment business. As we continued with our conversation, I could hear some small children in the background referring to him as grandpa. I asked him why he didn't claim his girlfriend's children. My father admitted that he had been a father figure to them for the majority of their lives but they were not his children. I reminded him that since he had raised those children, they were his children and his grandchildren. I told my father that I visited New York often and asked if I could meet his children in the very near future. He told me that it was possible. After that conversation with my father, he never talked to me again. I believe that my boldness scared him off. We lost contact with one another just as quickly as we had found each other.

I decided to go to New York to say my goodbyes to the Disappointment my father had brought me over the years. My daughter, Anne, and I traveled by airplane to Brooklyn to attend his funeral. Visiting New York was always a good time for us. My children once said that they really loved the East Coast because it provided them with a sense of peace and closeness to their biological father. He was born and raised in Newark, New Jersey. Anne and I had never been to Brooklyn, since on all our many trips to the city, we had never placed visiting Brooklyn on our to-do list. My father had resided in Brooklyn for many years after he and my mother separated.

Anne and I were easily able to find the funeral home by subway. As we walked the few block necessary to get to there, we realized that we had really missed a great opportunity. Brooklyn is a great city with lots of interesting things to do. When we arrived at the funeral home, there was no evidence that there would even be a funeral — it was empty. Anne and I were some of the first people to arrive.

It was very peaceful when we walked into the room where my father's services would be held, and I noticed that my father was going to be laid to rest in a beautiful white casket. I walked over to view his body before anyone else arrived. I found myself looking at a man who I didn't know. It had been over forty years since I had last seen my father, and he was now eighty-one years old. I didn't feel a sense of connection to the elderly white-haired gentleman who laid lifeless the white casket. Anne and I took a seat in the back of the room as we waited for the service to begin.

Prior to the start of the service, the pastor who spoke the eulogies instructed everyone to rise for the family's entrance. I instantly felt a sense of disconnect. The only people to my knowledge who were family members to the deceased were his niece, his granddaughter (Anne), and me. However, Anne and I weren't part of the entourage being referred to as *"The family"*. We stood up anyway to watch the endless entourage of *"family members"* pouring into the room. The entourage included all of my father's girlfriend's family. They all wore black and seemed to cry profusely. An immediate feeling of sadness and joy overcame me. I was sad that my father had died without affording my sister and me the opportunity to be a part of his life. In contrast, I felt joy in knowing that he'd had so many people who apparently had loved and cared about him.

I was disappointed to learn that my father had lied to me. As I reviewed his obituary, I noticed that there was a male's name on it listed as my father's son who lived in New Jersey. It was apparent that I had a younger brother. I could not believe my eyes, and I was furious that my father had kept the fact that I had a young brother from me. He'd robbed me of a relationship with my half-brother. I'd lived in New Jersey for nearly five years and had a younger brother I didn't know about who'd lived in a nearby city only a few miles away.

After my father's funeral, Anne and I quickly disappeared back into the streets of Brooklyn just as quickly as we'd arrived. I didn't want to stay around to rub elbows with my father's girlfriend's family. I considered introducing myself to her but quickly changed my mind. We took the subway back to Manhattan and enjoyed the remainder of our trip shopping and relaxing. I couldn't wait to get home to attempt contacting my half-brother. When I arrived home, I searched the Internet to see if I could find any information about him, and I decided to pay for his contact information through a people finder website.

I called the number that was provided by the finder service for my half-brother. A woman answered the telephone, and I said, "Hello, my name is Benita. Is Darryl home?"

The woman inquired about my reason for the call, and I told her, "I'm Clyde's daughter." She let down her guard and said, "Oh, yes, I remember you. I'm Darryl's mother. Your father spoke about you and your sister when Clyde and I were dating."

"I just attended his funeral, and that's where I learned that I had a half-brother," I replied.

It seemed like a big weight was lifted off her shoulders as we talked. The woman told me that Darryl was home and quickly went to get him. Darryl and I talked for at least an hour. We shared stories about how our father had come to bring us both DISAPPOINTMENTS.

I asked Darryl, "Why weren't you at the funeral?"

"We were never notified of his passing," he replied.

He was surprised to learn that his name was listed as his son on our father's obituary. He told me story after story of how our father hadn't been there for him. We decided to make an effort to keep in touch with each other, and we have since made good on that promise.

CHAPTER 31

Acceptance: Tension Everywhere

When I returned home, there was still a lot of tension between Terry and me. I believe that he was torn between the relationship he had with me and the one he had with his mother. It seemed like Terry was changing overnight. As he changed, so did his disposition; he became angry and started acting out his anger. His grades began to slowly decline. Suddenly, he also had behavioral problems at school, and he was showing the same propensity for behavioral issues as Marcus. The more Terry changed, the more I distanced myself from him. I didn't like the person he was becoming. It was easy for him to turn his anger toward me, especially since I was the only one willing to discipline him. Things really came to a head the day he asked me to switch his operable cell phone for a better one.

"Mom, can you switch my cell phone out for this one?" he asked.

"I'm not willing to do that," I replied.

I was the account holder, and I wasn't willing to do anything nice for him at that point. He'd betrayed our trust many times, and I still hadn't forgiven him. He didn't like my answer and decided to take matters into his own hands.

He asked my sister, "Do you know my mom's social security number?"

"Why do you ask?" she wondered.

My sister denied his request, so he asked his father to switch the cell phone, but Deon told him that he needed to ask me. When it became obvious that he wasn't going to get his way, he began calling the carrier himself, hoping to reach an agent who would make the change without my authority. When I came home that evening, my sister told me that he'd asked her for my social security number. I was furious! I called the cell phone carrier and asked if they had received any calls about my account. The agent confirmed that there were several calls made regarding accessing my account, so I went down to his room to confront him about the situation.

"Why are you going behind my back? I told you that I wouldn't switch the cell phone," I chastised him.

Terry lashed out at me. It was the first time I had ever seen him act in such an aggressive manner toward me. Terry was a few inches taller than me. He jumped up from his bed, and while towering over me, he attempted to entice me into a shouting match, but I did my best to remain claim. I certainly had no intention of allowing him the opportunity to become physical with me.

"You're not my mother, Benita!" he shouted. He continued to disrespect me by taunting me and calling me by my name several times.

I was thankful that I had been going to church. The Lord gave me peace over the chaos. Normally, I would have reacted to Terry's invitation. Deon was outside in the garage, talking to some friends, and he didn't have a clue that trouble was on the horizon. I went out to the garage to tell him that we had a problem needing his immediate attention. Terry had followed me out to the garage in an attempt to get his version of the episode heard. Deon attempted to calm Terry down, and he was annoyed that we were fighting. In Terry's anger, he attempted to cause tension between Deon and me.

"Why are you still with her? You don't even like her anymore. Why are you still with her? Why can't we live together?" he fired each question with more intensity than the first.

Deon attempted to calm him down. I went up to my room and decided not to worry about things, since I was confident that Deon would handle the situation appropriately. For Deon, Terry's rant was simply a teenager's angry words in the heat of the moment, but for me, they were something more sinister. Terry had placed a seed of doubt in my mind about my own marriage to his father. I began to wonder what he knew about my marriage that I didn't. I began to question Deon's feelings for me. Deon arranged for Terry to go over to Rita's house until things cooled off. I wasn't in favor of that decision, and I felt that it wasn't any of Rita's business what was going on in our house. We were capable of handling our own internal issues. Later that evening, Terry called from Rita's house, but that was odd, because Terry's cell phone wasn't working as a result of his tampering with it when he had attempted to have it switched to the other cell phone.

"How is Terry able to use his cell phone?" I asked.

What came out of Deon's mouth nearly floored me, "I called the cell phone carrier and instructed them to switch it," Deon reported with a stern tone.

I was livid. I wondered why he would contribute to Terry's mayhem. In my opinion, his actions were worse than Terry's. Deon should not have gone against me when Terry was clearly in the wrong. I began to rethink our relationship. There were some negative forces working against us, and they were clearly winning.

Deon and I never sat down with Terry to discuss the root cause for the blow-up, which was certainly a missed opportunity. Deon felt like he was in the middle of a war. He talked to Terry, but that really wasn't enough as far as I was concerned. From that point on, things between Terry and I changed. Things between Deon and I started to change, too.

After things died down, I questioned Deon about Terry's allegations, "Why did Terry say that you didn't like me anymore?" I asked. I wanted to gain some honest insight about why he had said those things.

"I can't justify Terry's actions," he replied.

I didn't like his answer, and it was a bit unsettling. I processed his lack of sensitivity as *"man-code"* or a son's loyalty to his father. The entire situation took a toll on me. I couldn't find acceptance for a child's disrespect for his father's marriage and a father being okay with it.

Deon and I went on with our lives, despite the problems. We decided to go back to school again, and we enrolled in a graduate program at Indiana Wesleyan University to obtain our Master's Degree in Business Administration. We contacted a family friend to see if she could babysit Leah one night a week while we attended school, and she agreed to help out.

Going back to school seemed to be a diversion, because it always allowed us the opportunity to re-group and take our mind off the stress of taking care of children and dealing with problems. That is, until our babysitter informed us that Rita was lurking around. Our babysitter lived next door to the church where Rita attended. It just so happened that the night we choose to go to school, Rita also attended some sort of activity there. Our babysitter understood and respected our unique circumstances regarding Rita and Leah, so she attempted to limit the time she allowed Leah and her children to play outside when Rita was around. Nonetheless, one day while she allowed the children to play at a nearby park across the street from her house, Rita and her mother drove by.

"Leah," she yelled out the window repeatedly.

It seemed like no matter what we did or where we went, Rita was always in the midst of things. We completed the majority of our Master's Degree program until our program was discontinued for members of management, but we were happy to have benefited from the educational benefits, and we almost completed three degrees.

It was 2008; the economy was making a turn for the worse, and Deon and I had some serious concerns about the future of the automotive industry. There were rumors circulating around the plant that for the first time in a long while members of management would be able to participate in the company buy-out program. We discussed our financial situation and weighed the pros and cons of my participating in the buyout. I believed that it would be the perfect opportunity for me to make a career change, so I continued to work, to attended church, and to take care my family while considering my options.

Prior to having a full appreciation of Facebook and its ability to link family and friends together instantly, I was enjoying another website called Classmates. I frequented the website as a means to reunite with some of the people I went to high school with back in San Diego. While on the website, one day I thought about James and wondered what he was doing with his life, so I sent him a brief message that read, *"How's life treating you? I know you probably have a wife and children. I just wanted to say hello."* At the time, I really had no expectation of getting a response from him. I didn't even think he frequented the websites, but I thought it was worth a shot to reach out to him.

After I sent the message, I checked the website a few times to see if I had a response. After I didn't hear anything back, I dismissed the idea that I would ever hear from him. I continued to use the website to talk to other people I went to high school with. I wanted to have some contact with the people from where I came from, especially since I didn't have any good friends in Kokomo. I needed an outlet that seemed normal to me. My addiction to dysfunction was getting the best of me, which was causing me to become depressed again.

My mother informed me that my Uncle Richard had passed away, so I decided to make the trip back to Killeen to attend his funeral. I was very excited to be going back to Killeen. My mother, sister, and some other family members were going to be there. We all wanted to say our goodbyes to my Uncle Richard. I had not seen my mother in a few years and wanted to surprise her.

"Don't tell my mama I'm coming out there," I pleaded to my Uncle Richard's son Richard.

"You can trust me, and I know everyone is going to be happy to see you," Richard said.

Anne, Leah, and I made the long, laborious drive from Kokomo to Killeen, Texas. We only had a day to get there, and we arrived in Killeen just in time for my Uncle Richard's funeral services. He received a full gun salute at his funeral since he had been in the military. After his funeral, I was happy to be reunited with my mother and to meet some cousins who I didn't know. I was especially thrilled to meet my Uncle Richard's son whose name is also Richard. We hit it off right away. He is about ten years younger than me, but I related to him very well. He has the most beautiful children. My cousin, Mary, wasn't able to attend her father's funeral because she was incarcerated. It felt really good to be around so much family at the same time. My Uncle Carl also came to the funeral from St. Louis. However, I did have some regrets that day. I had been holding in some anger toward my Uncle Richard for a few years and never took the opportunity to apologize or tell him that I loved him before he died.

"I really feel terrible," I told my cousin, Richard.

"Don't be so hard on yourself; we all had our moments with pops," he said.

I had a great sense of appreciation for my beautiful family. It bothered me that we were not close. As a child, I'd always yearned to be closer to my family. My mother was surprised that I had driven all the way to Killeen. We all had an enjoyable time. My cousin Richard and I were able to establish a closeness that would last. It was good to also see my sister and her family, too.

Back in Kokomo, the official news came down from the corporate office that the company buyout program was officially being extended to members of management. There was still a lot of uncertainly in the automobile industry, especially with the Big Three automakers.

I decided to take the buyout along with several other members of management within my department. Deon and I discussed how we would use some of the proceeds to pay off some debts. One of the enticing things that went into my decision was the $30,000 automobile voucher that was part of the buyout package. I took the company buyout, thus leaving the plant where I had worked for nearly fourteen years. It was certainly bittersweet, but we used our voucher to purchase a loaded Chrysler 300.

After I left the plant, I began to spend endless hours on Internet jobs boards searching for what I believed was going to be my dream job. I had no idea that the job market was saturated with jobs that paid very low wages. Here I was with an Associate's Degree, a Bachelor's Degree, and I was less than five classes away from obtaining a Master's Degree, but I was unable to secure a job that paid well. I

couldn't believe that there were no well-paying jobs that met my qualifications. I had failed to research the job market prior to leaving my employment at the plant, so I had to deal with the consequences. Those consequences further fueled my depression.

It was 2009; I secured a fulltime job as a case manager which required me to drive out of town for work daily. I liked the job, but I didn't like the compensation I received, and I began to live a pretty boring existence. My daily routine was typical; I went to work, came home, and took care of my daughter — all in that order.

My relationship with Deon was becoming distant. Our problems stemmed from various sources, which included my weight gain, my lack of interest in going anywhere, and my feelings about my home life. My feelings toward Deon were changing. He immersed himself in the motorcycle world, and it seemed like we didn't know each other anymore. There were significant communication issues on both our parts. We simply existed. Deon was taking full advantage of my not wanting to go anywhere with him, and he went out of town nearly every other weekend and rarely stayed home. He seemed to love the attention the motorcycle scene provided. Deon is pretty confident in his physical looks, and to put it frankly, *"My husband simple thinks he's cute!"*

We had always been able to mask our personal problems with each other because we always had so many other distractions. I slowly began to unplug from everything and everyone I knew, and my addiction to dysfunction was taking a turn for the worse. I developed a case of the old-maid syndrome and wanted to stay home all the time. I turned to food to comfort myself and gained a considerable amount of weight. I noticed that I had gained nearly twenty pounds soon after leaving the plant. I had never realized how much exercise I was getting as I ran all over the plant to resolve multiple issues. My demons were returning to plague me, and I definitely let myself go. Something was very wrong with my marriage, but I couldn't put my finger on it. I wasn't attending church as often as I should, and without the benefit of spiritual covering, it was easy for me to allow outsides forces to drain me physically and emotionally. Meanwhile, Deon was becoming just as frustrated with me as I was with him.

CHAPTER 32

Acceptance: An Accident Can Bring Awareness

In May of 2009, I received a telephone call from Deon's brother, David, informing me that Deon had a motorcycle accident, "You need to get to the hospital quick," he reported.

"How bad is it?" I inquired.

"We don't know yet," he replied.

It was so surreal. It was only nineteen years earlier that I had received the same type of news about Antoine being shot, and I didn't know what to expect, so I quickly grabbed my belongings and headed to the hospital. While driving to the hospital, my mind ran rampant with negative thoughts. I braced myself for the news that would come. It seemed like the short walk from my car to the entrance of the hospital took forever, and I walked up to the information desk to inquire about Deon's whereabouts.

"I'm here to see my husband Deon," I said.

The clerk told me he was still in the Triage Unit, and I was taken back to see him. Deon was lying in his hospital bed with his left leg elevated and in bandages. The attending nurse told me that he'd broken his left leg. At first it did not appear that his injuries were all that serious. The nurse took several X-rays and waited for the doctor to interpret them. About two hours later, a doctor came in and explained to Deon that he had broken several bones in his left leg. The doctor further explained that he needed to be transported to another hospital that was more equipped to handle these types of injuries, so Deon provided the hospital staff with his written consent to be transferred to another hospital and was transported by ambulance to a hospital in Indianapolis that night.

"Can I ride down to Indy with my husband?" I inquired.

The ambulance driver said I couldn't ride along in the ambulance, but he suggested that I follow along in my personal vehicle.

It was very dark and rainy out that night. The visibility was nearly impossible, and it was hard for me to keep up with the ambulance since the driver drove at least eighty miles an hour, leaving me to find my own way there. When Deon arrived at the hospital, he was admitted, and I stayed overnight at the hospital with him since we were under the impression that he would have emergency surgery that night.

The next morning, a doctor arrived and told Deon, "You have a pretty nasty break. We plan to have surgery tomorrow."

I couldn't believe that Deon had been so irresponsible at the drag strip, and I wasn't very happy with him. Deon had been building a high-performance racing motorcycle for nearly a year and was finally finished with his project motorcycle and ready to race it. He wanted to prove to the motorcycle community that he was still the fastest drag-strip racer in town, so he had taken his race bike to the drag strip that day to test and tune it for the upcoming racing season. Deon had added some nitrous gas to gain additional speed, but in the process he had added too much. That was a grave mistake. He realized that it could be problematic but decided to ignore his intuition, so he lined his race bike up and positioned himself to make a pass down the track. When the green light came on indicating that it was time to go, he gunned the throttle. As Deon made the pass down the track, his race bike went airborne with him at the helm. His bike landed on top of him causing his left leg to make substantial contact with the hard gravel road, and Deon shattered several bones in his left knee. The pit crew along with the drag strip employees rushed over to assist him.

Deon's doctor planned to secure his left leg by using an outside device to straighten it as part of his first surgical procedure, as it was imperative that his leg be straightened before any additional surgeries could be preformed. His doctor made a horrendous error by keeping the outside device on his left leg a few weeks longer than was necessary, and, as a result, Deon develop a blood clot in his left leg from it being in one position too long. Consequently, several things spiraled out of control with his care. In all, Deon was required to have at least six surgical procedures resulting from the accident.

We took issue with the hospital regarding all the mistakes that were made, only to be given excuses for why his doctors had made the decisions. During the majority of the time, Deon was bedridden. For months he lay in a hospital bed in our living room unable to care for himself. It was a very difficult time for him, but I took good care of him throughout his illness and nursed him back to health. I partnered with him and played a substantial role in his recovery.

I learned a lot about Deon during his downtime that really bothered me. Some of the female riders seemed to know him better than I thought they did, and it seemed that he had made a few *"new"* friends. They had been hanging around and going on rides with his motorcycle group. Some of those females made appearances at the hospital, and I wondered if he had a fan club I wasn't aware of. For many of them, it was their first time meeting me, and some of them already knew me but hadn't seen me in a while.

"Since when did you get so damn friendly with these females?" I asked him.

"They're just biker chicks," he replied.

I wasn't a frequent visitor to the motorcycle scene, and I had given the "hussies" full reign of my husband. The "out of sight, out of mind" rules applied. I'd always preferred to stay at home with our children instead of running the streets. A few of the females even had the audacity to drop by our house on several occasions to bring Deon food and other necessities, and I became consumed with anger. When I discussed my concerns with Deon, he dismissed them and failed to understand my point of view. He didn't *want* to understand! It bothered me that not only did the females seem comfortable around him, but he seemed comfortable around them, too. I was really caught off guard. I have always given him a lot of space, and it never bothered me that he wanted to ride his motorcycle that he loves to ride. It is his favorite pastime. I wholeheartedly believe that both parties in a marriage should allow each other some space to do the things they enjoy doing, and I was always under the impression that he was out riding and racing motorcycles with his male companions. Deon was fully aware that my only concern with him being out riding was that he kept a high level of respect for me. I asked him what had changed in our relationship that had caused him to show a disregard for our relationship. I didn't feel that it was appropriate for him to be that friendly with those women, and I began to wonder what was going on when he wasn't at home.

Deon assured me that those females were just part of a female motorcycle club who enjoyed riding with other motorcycle clubs. He further explained that they were simply showing their support for their injured motorcycle brother, but I didn't buy his explanation. I told him that I had a problem with them coming around. It wasn't a case of jealous on my part. I just wanted Deon to show me the same consideration that he would expect from me. If the shoe were on the other foot, his temper would have hit the roof. There was no way I could have gotten away with such nonsense. The first man who would have walked up to our door to deliver me food would have been the last. I reminded Deon that I was his wife and was fully capable and responsible for taking care of his needs, but he seemed to love the attention he was receiving. I eventually let down my guard and became friendly with most of the female riders after they started to respect my space.

The longer it took for Deon to recover from his motorcycle accident, the more bitter he became, especially toward his friends and family. Deon was particularly disappointed with Marcus and Terry. They were absent throughout his downtime which made him furious.

"I can't believe my damn kids haven't even come over to check on me," he complained.

"Don't worry about it. Just focus on getting better," I would advise him.

Terry made a few appearances to get a dollar or two but never stayed long. Deon always supported them and expected them to be by his side during his time of need. He felt that none of his children were there for him the way he imagined they would be. His daughter, Ty, made some appearances while he was in the hospital, but as the months passed, it seemed like no one was coming over to visit him except for his brother David and his father.

Deon was surprised how much his father was there for him. His father displayed a level of concern that went a long way toward healing their strained relationship. Deon did all he could to remind some key individuals who he really wanted to see while he was bedridden. He would call or text them to garner a response from them. Once he reached a high level of frustration, he went on a rant that consisted of rude and sarcastic comments about them. The more his friends and family ignored his wishes, the worse his attitude became. It was apparent to him that the only people around for him were Rasheed, Anne, Kashif, Leah, and I. Between the five of us, we took good care of him during his yearlong downtime period.

Deon was able to rekindle his once strained relationship with his cousin Richard, but he became angry with the world after his motorcycle accident and I somehow became the recipient of the majority of his frustration. It was very hard for him to stay in the house and relax, and he was not enjoying his downtime very well.

In my mind, I believed that Deon's accident had brought us closer. We were spending a lot of time praying for his healing, watching television, and enjoying each other's company. However, Deon was entertaining some very different thoughts about our relationship than I was. His anger toward me intensified when I didn't make myself available to him around the clock.

Deon couldn't walk for the majority of the time and was confined to his hospital bed, and I went up to bed nightly around eleven o'clock. Prior to retiring to bed, I would ask him if he needed anything, and once Deon said he had everything he needed, I went to bed, since I had to make sure that I got enough rest prior to going to work the following day.

Deon perceived my not being available 24/7 as me being mean to him. I believe that he was going through a period of isolation and was afraid to be abandoned. Although I was withholding some anger against him because of the issues with the female friends, I never let him down throughout the ordeal. I was annoyed with him when he

186

acted like a brat as he often does, but I did my best to take care of him while working fulltime. When it was time for Deon to return back to work at the plant, he went on the midnight shift, but he still had some substantial mobility issues, and we both had some unresolved anger toward one another.

Deon returned to the motorcycle life he'd had prior to his accident. He resumed his frequent visits to the motorcycle clubs, going out of town, and spending a lot of time away from home. He'd lost a significant amount of weight after his accident and was looking better than he had in years. Of course, with the weight loss came even more female attention.

CHAPTER 33

Forgiveness: Just Stopping By

I decided to go back to school to obtain a Graduate Certificate in Human Resources, and my program required me to take a few online classes. As a result, I was spending a lot of time on the Internet. One December afternoon while I was checking my personal emails, I noticed that there was an email from the Classmates website. It seemed like the email jumped right off the page, prompting me to open it. I was curious, so I opened it right away. The email's content was very beautiful and meaningful and really struck a cord with me. The email was from James. He had resurfaced to ask for FORGIVINESS for the pain he had caused me some thirty years earlier. He was undoubtedly referring to the child we had agreed to abort. I was taken aback and surprised to hear from him, and I was very impressed and touched that he had the courage to ask for my forgiveness. James apologized for not stepping up and being the man he should have been. I could tell by his tone how much he deeply regretted his role in my having an abortion. He was truly sorry. The email was cathartic. It helped to release me from the guilt that I also felt. I wanted everyone that was

189

close to me to know about the meaningful email I had received from him, so I told a few people, including Deon, about it. I bragged about how meaningful the email from James was to me. Deon was already aware of our decision to abort our child some thirty-something years earlier.

"Deon, I got the sweetest email from James apologizing," I said, but he didn't show any support either way.

He basically blew off the news of my email as unimportant, which I thought was rude. James' email began to stir a deep desire in me to want to talk to him. I wanted to hear him verbally reiterate those beautiful words to me, so I decided to reply back to thank him for sending the beautiful email. I was going to give him the forgiveness he asked for.

It was 2010; I was still working on my graduate HR certificate. I was attending classes one night a week and working a part-time job in town. I was feeling pretty defeated! Everything in my life seemed to be out of order. I didn't have any inner-peace. I received a call from a friend telling me about a possible job lead as a supervisor with a major company. I was excited to learn about the position, so I submitted my resume to the company and was called for an interview. The possibility of obtaining a fulltime position again gave Deon and me something positive to focus on. My working part-time was causing a strain on our family budget, but just when I believed the tide was turning, I found out that the company decided to go with another candidate. I was devastated because I really wanted to get back into a supervisory role. The position was going to be a great fit. I was really in a rut. Deon and I continued to live our lives, but the gap in distance between us was widening.

In was March 2010; Deon sent me on a much-needed mini-trip to New York, and my daughter, Anne, was able to take some time off from work to accompany me. I love going on mini-vacations with Anne, as she always makes me feel better. Anne is my rock! When I boarded the airplane, I began to experience a panic attack, and I was devastated to learn that I could barely buckle the seatbelt. I knew my hips had expanded more than I would have liked them to, but I never thought I would find myself wrestling to buckle a seatbelt. I struggled to secure the already-extended seatbelt around my hips. My heart sank as I pulled and tugged the seatbelt while attempting to secure it. Anne was seated in another section of the airplane and was oblivious to the torture I was going through. There I sat, alone and humiliated, as I continued to try to fasten my seatbelt.

As the flight attendant proceeded with the mandatory safety demonstration, I silently cried out to God. I asked Him to help me to fasten my seatbelt. I was so afraid that I was going to be asked to leave the plane, or worse, required to purchase an additional seat. I didn't want to be ostracized and labeled as the "fat lady" on the flight. God was with me, and as I prayed, I was finally able to fasten my seatbelt and to breathe a sigh of relief. It was yet another one of the worse days of my life.

When Anne and I arrived in New York, I noticed that I wasn't having the great time I was accustomed to. I was finding it difficult to get around the city without getting tuckered out.

"I need a break," I told Anne.

"Mom, I told you to start putting yourself first," she said. Now she was *my* mother.

I was faced with the reality that I had really let myself go physically, and I needed to make some changes once I returned home. I realized that I needed to lose some weight, so I began doing some light activities such as walking around the neighborhood to address my weight issues, and it was beginning to work.

One day I was checking the Classmates website to see if James had responded to the email I sent him, and I was shocked to find that he had responded. We began corresponding with emails through the website. Initially, we simply caught up on the events from the past thirty years, and we had a lot of catching up to do. One of the things James told me was that he had never had any biological children of his own. He was married and still lived in California. I told him I had not been there in years but that my mother still lived there. We reminisced about the good-old times when we first met during my cheerleading days. Over the next few months, our feelings began to strengthen for one another. In many ways, it seemed like no time had passed between us. The more Deon unplugged, the closer James and I became.

I dreaded the thought of James seeing me since I wasn't slim anymore. I enjoyed his company, and it was nice to be in contact with someone from back home. The more I chatted with James, the more suspicious Deon became.

I started to place more emphasis on myself and my needs. I considered how embarrassed I would be if James or anyone from my past was to see the way I had let myself go. I wasn't the 5'6", 125 pound cheerleader they remembered, so I started walking every day. Initially, I was walking to gain the acceptance of other people, but the more I exercised, the more I started doing it for myself. I enjoyed being outside, taking in the fresh air and soaking up sunshine as I walked. I liked the emotional place I was in and the peace that went along with it. I was rebirthing myself and was beginning to let go of past hurts and offenses that had once plagued me.

I began using Facebook to connect with friends. One of them who had once lived in Newark told me that he was friends with Kenny and that he really wanted to reconnect with me, so I searched Facebook and sent Kenny a friend request. He was very happy to hear that I was doing well and told me that over the years he often worried about me and my children.

"Good to hear from you. How are the kids?" he inquired.

"They're all doing well. They went to college, and I'm so proud of them," I bragged. I was able to forgive Kenny, and I released the anger I had held against him for Antoine's death years earlier.

I wanted to gain a better understanding about Antoine's death, since it was coming up on the 20th anniversary. Over the years, my children had expressed an interest in wanting to know the concrete details of their father's death, so I wanted to make sure I cleared up as many of their concerns as possible.

"What really happened on that horrific day?" I inquired, and Kenny was more than willing to cooperate.

Kenny talked for over an hour about the ordeal, and I communicated his account of events to my children. It gave us all a sense of closure. I'd never had the opportunity to grieve Antoine's death, nor had I allowed myself to forgive the person who was responsible for his murder. I was really happy that Kenny reached out to me, and we have remained friends on Facebook. I'm very proud of his life's accomplishments, since he is now a well-established chef in New York.

Deon became suspicious and began asking me if I was talking to someone on the computer.

"Are you talking to someone inappropriately on your computer?" he investigated.

"No, I told you I wasn't," I replied. I quickly played things down by telling him I was talking to the same friends I'd always had on Facebook.

There were occasions when he ignored some of the other red flags which indicated that something was wrong. I had become distant, and Deon was still running the streets. The only thing we seemed to have in common was our love for our grandchildren. We enjoyed visiting Marcus to see his children and often did special things with them. Visiting our grandchildren kept us connected.

It was the summer of 2010; Deon was acting very illusive. For the first time in our relationship, he started acting aggressively toward me, and it was almost like living with a bully. Upon his return from the various trips he went on, he came home looking for anything he could find to argue about. His tone and demeanor was different, so I simply tuned him out and decided not to feed into his drama. My children were seeing me through the difficult period, and I began to seriously consider leaving Kokomo. I wasn't happy, but I was obligated to stay to complete my HR program.

Deon's actions were driving a wedge between us, and something was definitely going on with him. Our feelings were changing toward each other, but we didn't know how to communicate them to the other person, and we continued to allow things to stay on their destructive path.

Reconnecting with James made me feel alive again, and I began changing some of my self-destructive behaviors, especially my problems with food and isolating myself. I traded those behaviors for healthier ones, and I stopped being a homebody and began getting out more. My daughter, Anne, really came to my aid by doing what she could to make me feel good about myself, "Mom, let's go get our hair done," she'd say.

She treated me to get my hair and nails done regularly. It was her way of rescuing me from myself. It seemed like God sent James to save me also. His return appearance wasn't only for him to seek forgiveness but also to show me how to forgive myself. He brought to my remembrance the person he remembered, "Hey, I remember the girl with the beautiful heart," he'd say to encourage me. I really appreciated everything James brought to the conversation.

It became apparent that things between Deon and I had reached a new low when we both forgot to wish each other a happy 17th anniversary. Our anniversary and my birthday were both in the same month, and my birthday celebration was also a lackluster event. Over the years, Deon had always showered me with beautiful gifts, like diamonds or other things of sentimental value. Our marriage was in trouble, and Deon was becoming paranoid. I really wanted to escape the reality of my broken marriage by running away to Killeen. Unbeknownst to me, he was secretly wishing that he would come home one day and I'd be gone.

One summer afternoon, Deon had a meltdown. I'd never seen him act like that before. He was an emotional wreck when he confronted me, "You don't love me anymore," he said.

"I do," I said.

I did still love him, but I was disappointed in the direction our marriage was taking. I wanted to be as honest as I could with him regarding my feelings, but I decided to soothe him. I wasn't ready to tackle our problems while he was in such a vulnerable state of mind.

I prayed a lot about our marriage, asking God to give me the courage to be honest with Deon, and God gave me exactly what I asked for. After a few days passed, I engaged him in a conversation.

"We need to talk," I asserted.

"About what?" he asked.

I began to reveal my true feelings to him — I told him that I believed it would best if we went our separate ways. I assured him that I would always love him and wanted to remain good friends. Our conversation was long overdue, and it was as if a big weight was being lifted off my shoulders. After Deon digested everything I said, he gave me his point of view. We realized that we had missed a lot of opportunities to be a loving partner to one another, and after our candid conversation, we decided that our marriage was worth fighting for and renewed our commitment to stay together.

I contacted James in California immediately to inform him of the conversation I'd had with Deon. James and I were communicating daily, and he wasn't ready to give up our newly-rekindled relationship. There were over two thousand miles between us, but we managed to have some pretty steady interactions.

"Okay, but you have to promise that you will pray about things," James said.

"I promise, and thank you," I replied.

I attempted to get things back on track, and I appreciated James, since he never tried to tear Deon down like most men do when they are invading their territory. James and I established early on in our relationship that the one thing we didn't want to do was hurt our spouses. We realized that we were being selfish by having a secret relationship, but we had a strong emotional connection from our past. He wished me well, and we vowed to always remain good friends.

Within days of relinquishing my secret relationship with James, Deon resumed the same behaviors he vowed to stop after our talks of reconciliation. He began making plans to go out of town and started running the streets again. I couldn't believe that he was acting this way, so my feelings were hurt and my trust for him went right out the window.

I immediately reached out to James, "James, I need you to talk to me," I pleaded.

"Go back to your husband," he advised.

He was very angry with me and started ignoring my texts. He believed that I was playing with his feelings. James and I never ask the other to leave their marriage. He decided to forgive me and we resumed daily talks. Over the course of six months, James asked for my forgiveness several times for his actions some thirty years earlier, since he had really been emotionally affected by the ordeal, and together we were able to find closure for our decision to terminate our child. I found a great appreciation for the man who now he is. However, we were definitely playing with fire. During the course of our talks, we never saw one another with the exception of a picture or two. However, our emotional connection was getting stronger, and someone was going to get burned!

It was becoming a pattern, and I was happy when Deon ran the streets, since my cell phone kept me company as I exchanged messages with James. I continued to entertain thoughts of moving to Killeen to start a new life, while Deon and I were not treating each other well and our marriage was losing its footing. We were become glorified roommates, and I was becoming so comfortable texting James that I really didn't care if I got caught. One night, while Deon was out late, James was keeping me company. I didn't have to go anywhere special to have my emotional affair, but when Deon returned home that night and crawled into bed, I was very restless.

I was unable to sleep, so I reached out to James. When he texted me back, I began engaging in yet another conversation with him. I honestly believed that Deon had fallen asleep, since he was doing his usual loud snoring. I continued texting James into the wee hours of the morning. There was a three-hour time difference, but we developed a schedule as to when it was best to talk. To my surprise, Deon sensed that I was up to no good, as my cell phone continued to illuminate in the darkness with each incoming text while Deon lay there playing possum.

The next thing that happened was the unthinkable; Deon jumped out of the bed and began screaming at the top of his lungs at me, "You can go live with the bastard you're texting!" he proclaimed.

He attempted to get my cell phone away from me while demanding to know who I was talking to. I couldn't believe what was happening, and I didn't know what to. I was busted. At that point, I wasn't going to lie to him.

"I'm talking to a friend," I yelled out.

"What friend?" he demanded.

He grabbed my cell phone from me and attempted to read my messages. In retrospect, it was really pretty amusing to watch him frantically attempting to learn the what, who, when, where, and how of my actions, but he was able to view the last text I had sent to James, and he didn't like what he read. I was ashamed and couldn't believe that I had disrespected him. Deon was furious and asked for an immediate divorce, and I certainly wasn't going to argue with him. By this time, everyone in the house could hear the ruckus. I never wanted to put my children or husband through this, but Deon had the right to ask for a divorce. I couldn't blame my actions on anyone but myself, and although James and I had not seen or touched each other in over thirty years, we were both guilty of emotionally cheating on our spouses. That was a personal issue we would both have to ask God for forgiveness in prayer.

Deon didn't say a word to me for at least thirty minutes. In his silence, I began to do some soul-searching. I asked myself if I really wanted a divorce. My oldest son Rasheed told me that he wouldn't respect me if I didn't do all I could to make my marriage work. I was proud to have raised such an insightful young man.

"I don't want a divorce," I told Deon.

"Leave me the hell alone," he lashed out in anger.

I wondered if Deon and I could really find acceptance for one another and have a respectful marriage. I believed that this was just one of those tests that married couples have to endure to get to where they need to be. No one ever said that marriage would be easy. It takes a commitment to honesty from both sides to make things work. The number one priority in a marriage has to be spending quality time with each other, but Deon and I weren't doing that.

My mother once gave me a critical piece of advice. She said, "If your husband ask you to go somewhere with him — go." Somewhere in our marriage, I had stopped taking her advice.

I assured Deon that if he wanted a divorce I would give him one. He needed to get as far away from me as possible to digest the drama that played out. I made peace with the fact that our marriage could possibly be over. I had just secured a full-time job out of town, and I decided to go ahead and start working since I needed to save some money. I certainly wasn't going to continue living in Kokomo if we weren't together, so I talked to James and told him how things had hit the fan between Deon and me. We knew at some point that our emotional relationship would have to end, and he understood that I was in a tight spot. We never intended to hurt anyone. It just felt good having someone to listen to me and support me.

CHAPTER 34

Acceptance: Putting the Pieces Back Together

After a few hours Deon called me; he wanted to talk. I felt responsible for breaking his heart. It was out of character for me, since I had never stepped out in our marriage prior to James' return. Deon and I talked about our marriage for hours. He hinted that he was falling out of love with me just as fast as I was with him. Our problems stemmed from the distance we both had allowed to seep into our marriage. Somehow, our seventeen-year marriage had hit a major roadblock.

"I love you, babe. I don't want a divorce," Deon said. He told me that he never wanted to live without me.

"I'm not ready to walk away from seventeen years of marriage either," I assured him.

We had experienced some missed steps in our marriage, but we had always been best friends, and we both wanted to get back those special moments we once shared. We had to put aside our own selfish agendas, and we also needed to consider how a divorce would affect our teenaged daughter, our adult children, and our seven grandchildren. Deon and I decided to put the spark back in our marriage. We both really wanted to, and he asked me to cut off all contact with James. I believed his request was reasonable. I didn't want to be a hypocrite, since if the shoe was on the other foot, I would want the same respect. I was grateful for the opportunity I had with James. He was really looking forward to getting back in church, and our emotional affair had served as a distraction for him as well.

It was 2011; Deon and I spent New Year's Eve at the wedding of some friends, and Deon was selected to be the best man. I thought that being in the presence of *"new love"* was the perfect way for us to bring in the New Year. The wedding symbolized new beginnings, not only for them but for us, too.

We both made a commitment to work hard to get our marriage back on track, and I noticed right away that Deon was making a stellar effort. Our communication with each other improved greatly, and we began to go on regularly-scheduled dates as a means to spend alone time together to keep our marriage balanced. Many of our dates included eating out a lot, which brought us happiness and also weight gain from all the frequent visits to restaurants. Over the course of a few months, Deon's insecurities would often win the day. He was having a difficult time trusting me. It was difficult to find acceptance for the fact that his beautiful wife had an emotional affair with a man she had not seen in over thirty years.

"It's so easy for women to have emotional affairs when they feel they aren't being paid attention to by their partners," I told him.

"Yeah, but you haven't seen that dude in thirty years," he reminded me.

I took full responsibility for my actions, and I was sensitive about Deon's feelings. It's never a good feeling when one spouse betrays the other's trust. However, it is possible to fall in love all over again if the effort is there.

Deon and I are relearning how to appreciate the simple things that originally attracted us to one another, such as the joy of laughter, going to concerts, comedy shows, movies, and visiting our grandchildren. Deon is making an effort to be a good husband to me. It warms my heart to see his face light up with his beautiful smile. I can tell that he feels loved again. I never stopped loving him; I just needed him to stand up for me, honor my feelings, and respect me. He is a good man with a loving heart. I love it when he dances in the "buff" for me and makes me laugh until it hurts. We truly have something special, and we have put the broken pieces back together in our marriage. Deon asked me to "stop allowing my mind to work against him" and I am making a great effort to honor his request.

We have refocused our attention to taking care of our daughter, Leah. We are certainly grateful that God entrusted us with her care, and our influence is helping her to become a beautiful young lady. Although we haven't changed our mind about Rita's involvement in her life, we have learned that God is the author and finisher of how their relationship will play out.

We are no longer threatened by Rita. Just as Deon and my relationships has gotten back on the right track, my relationship with other individuals has strengthened as well. I have learned to forgive Marcus and Terry, too. As a token of my forgiveness, I prepared for them a memory book to highlight our journey through life together over the years. The memory book serves as a token of my love for both of them. It also serves as a memoir of their lives and the care I provided for them in their mother's absence. Marcus was very happy to receive the memory book and was very emotional as he flipped through the pages. It really touched my heart. Terry also seemed to appreciate the memory book.

While I was on the road to bridging gaps in broken relationships, God spoke to my heart again. He told me that it was time to forgive Rita. I also needed to forgive her to achieve my own healing, so I honored His request. She has come a long way; God has taken her from glory to glory. She is a living testimony that anyone can conquer life's hard knocks. She is now gainfully employed and has made restitution to Deon for the back child support payments she once owed him, which was a step in the right direction. Rita was receptive to my forgiveness and asked for my forgiveness in the process. We can now move out of the past and into the future. I'm not sure what a future relationship will look like for us, but it feels good to be obedient when God speaks.

CHAPTER 35

Close the Door and Don't Look Back!

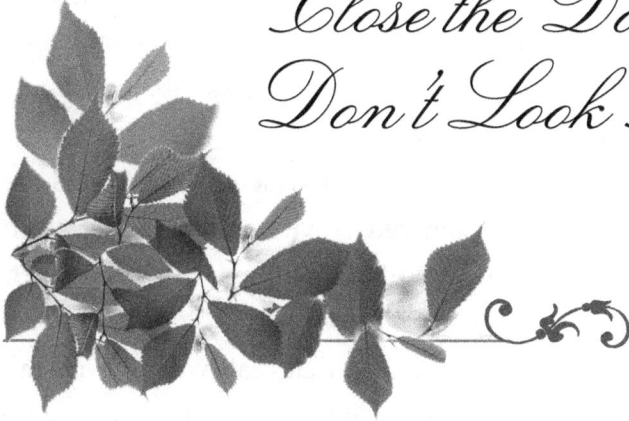

In life, we all face some form of dysfunction. Many of us are part of the walking wounded and are hanging on by a thread, but we just keep trying to get by in life. That is how we become addicted to dysfunction. Since most of us don't have the ability to self-diagnosis, when we realize that something is afoot, we become afraid to admit it and don't seek the help we need. Misery seeks misery, while pain and heartache becomes the backdrop of our lives. We must learn to create a different canvas. God's mercies are new every day. Just one seed can create a new seed, and we can break free from our addiction to dysfunction. In doing so, we can begin to live life out loud again.

Although disappointments are never easy to understand, we have to accept the fact that they are just part of life. There are countless numbers of children who grow up in both motherless and fatherless homes, due to no fault of their own. As a child, it is difficult to process why disappointments happen. The truth of the matter is, there are a thousand reasons why. Therefore, when we are no longer a child, we must have the courage to ask the parent or person who caused us disappointment *"their"* account of the story. We are often provided secondhand stories that become watered-down versions of the truth. Consequentially, we then transformed them into *"poor me"* stories followed by our excuse to live a *"pity party"* existence. Once we garner up enough courage to ask the hard questions of others, only then will we be able to accept the truth from whom we ask the questions. That is the moment when we can be free.

I thank God for my mother. She never provided my sister and me with any secondhand stories or watered down versions of the truth just to soothe us. In fact, she never badmouthed my father, not even after his death. My father simply didn't live with us — *"End of story."* We didn't spend a lot of time focusing on that reality. However, my disappointment came from my own experiences and interactions with my father. I had the right to experience disappointment when he never visited us, when he didn't make an honest attempt to get to know me while we visited him in St. Louis, or even when he used me for his own personal agenda to divorce my mother. As disappointing as all those things were to me, I learned a lot about myself. I am resilient and a natural born leader who God uses to edify others. I developed a strong sense of independence and tenacity. I have the character that many people would hope for.

My take on Disappointment is that I really didn't need to be disappointed in my father at all. Although I really didn't know a lot about him, I bet he experienced some brokenness in his life, too. Perhaps he was just another one of the walking wounded doing the best he could in life. It is possible that he died just as disappointed as I was. He may have been plagued by the same things that plague me. It is plausible that my father made mistakes, just like everyone else. I learned that once I placed my eyes on my Heavenly Father, He healed my hurts and allowed me to see that He had never left or forsaken me. My Father has been with me all the time. Because of that I forgive my earthy father.

We live in a free country; therefore, we are presented with a lot of choices. Some of the biggest choices in life are associated with the choosing of a mate. In spite of this, we don't always make the right choice. One of the hidden reasons for our error is that we allow fear to drive our choices. Fear is a powerful phenomenon. We don't want to live a life alone, so we get stuck in relationships that do not honor our true being. We don't take the time to really get to know the person of our choosing. Therefore, our relationship choices become compromised.

I've repeated the lesson of a poor choice in men more than once. However, my mother taught my sister and me one of the biggest lessons about relationship choices that a mother can pass on to her daughters. That lesson is; if a man's generosity doesn't match his character, he simply isn't worth the trouble. My mother's choice was a man who was a good provider but had abusive tendencies. However, she also had the courage to leave him. What a powerful lesson! As a result, I never chose a partner for money or materialistic things. I also vowed to never be in a physically abusive relationship. This lesson has been passed on to my beautiful daughters. I'm sure that John was yet another broken man with his own crosses to bear. Perhaps he came from a family who had a history of abuse. Perhaps he was addicted to dysfunction and didn't know how to get free. It is possible that he watched his own father's jealousy spin out of control with his mother. Perhaps, no one ever told John that his behavior was wrong. Because of that I forgive him.

"So, what gives you the right to ask for forgiveness?" Well... the answer to that question is God. He requires us to forgive others and is delighted when we forgive quickly. Forgiveness is not for the other person — it's for us. Show me a man or woman who doesn't need to be forgiven in at least one area of their life. At some point, we have to develop the courage to ask for forgiveness. The consequence of not asking can torment a person for life. Learning how to forgive also builds character. It took me some years to personally learn the power of forgiveness and to reap the benefits for doing so.

When James didn't want to have our child some thirty years ago, my immediate internal response was non-forgiveness. My avoidance of James served as a defense mechanism to forget him instead of forgive him. It could very well be that he took so long to ask for forgiveness from me because he harbored un-forgiveness toward me for caving in to his selfish wishes. It's also possible that James found it difficult to forgive himself. Nevertheless, his delay in asking for forgiveness cost him many years of anguish. I'm grateful that God requires us to forgive one another. James' request for forgiveness brought a sense of peace for the both of us. I falsely believed that I had made peace with the situation years ago, but I was wrong. Deep down in the core of my being, I needed the lesson James came to teach me. He needed the forgiveness that he received from me. It is possible that he feared being rejected by me the same way he had rejected me in our youth. James told his wife that one day he would have to ask for my forgiveness — it was just that important to him. Perhaps, all those many years ago, we should have had an open discussion about our decision to terminate our child, but I didn't know how. It's possible that James just needed time to grow up, and because of that I forgive him.

As consumers, we spend hours and hours researching data to make sure our purchases are acceptable to our lifestyles and preferences. However, when it comes to taking the steps necessary to ensure that the individuals whom we accept as life partners are right for us, we fail to do so. We jump right in relationships with our eyes shut, and we fail to protect our hearts. Having someone to love becomes our main goal, and we lose awareness. Nonetheless, we should make choosing a life partner just as important as making material purchases. I believe that the same types of background tests that are administered to candidates seeking employment should be utilized for finding life partners as well.

If we truly took the time to learn just the basic information about a person, we would save ourselves a lot of problems in the long run. God has equipped us with an internal alarm system called intuition. It's that little voice that goes off in our heads alerting us to negative conditions. Those red flags are often overridden and replaced by our own interpretation of things. I received a lot of red flags during my five-year marriage to Antoine. In the beginning, I was so happy to have his adoration that I jumped right into our marriage after only six months of knowing him. I was basically doing an on-the-job training exercise. I found out early on that we were too young for the jobs we had signed up for, and we simply didn't meet the job requirements. We also failed to read the job description for marriage and failed to ask couples who modeled such successes. I created a picture of the job duties for my husband in my mind based on a false reality. Television has a way of helping us do that. We are subjected to perfect characters who have perfect lives — well… at least they did when I watched *Leave it to Beaver*, and *The Brady Bunch*. However, those television husbands don't exist in real life.

Is it fair to convict a person for not living up to a false reality? I set Antoine up to fail right from the onset. I set the bar way too high based on my unrealistic awareness of what a real marriage between a nineteen and a twenty-one year old was suppose to be. In reality, it looks just like the one I had, especially if the individuals are not financially stable or mature. Perhaps Antoine loved me with all his heart and was doing the best he could as my husband, and perhaps I needed to turn off the television and read some books about marriage. The truth is, I loved Antoine just as much as he loved me. If I'd had a better awareness that he was broken and suffering from dysfunction, I could have been more sensitive. My take on awareness is that despite all that we went through, we created three beautiful children who I'm truly grateful to have in my life, Rasheed, Anne, and Kashif. Because of that I forgive him.

What does it mean to really accept others? We all know, without a doubt, that accepting others isn't easy. In fact, the person who we rarely find "true" acceptance for is ourselves. On the flip side of the coin, we often accept the behaviors of others that we simply shouldn't. Self-correction cannot be achieved if negative behaviors are not addressed. When we accept things, either good or bad, we have to own up to the decisions we make.

I wholeheartedly accepted Deon and his children. I'm that motivator you want in your corner when you're fighting your last round in the most important bout of your life. However, it was difficult for me to find acceptance for the majority of challenges we faced. In trying to help Deon raise his children, I learned that I wasn't prepared to face all the harsh criticism and attacks that came with raising a blended family. I wanted to do the right thing, which was to love my husband and his children. I made myself available to them as soon as I was aware that they needed my assistance. It was second nature for me to jump right in, and I did the best I could to care for Marcus and Terry in their mother's absence.

When children are living in a cycle of dysfunction due to no fault of their own, they are often exposed to things, such as *drug abuse, abandonment, manipulation, and destruction.* It is difficult to face all those things without the benefit of professional help. Perhaps Marcus and Terry were simply victims of their parent's ugly divorce. It is likely that they craved the positive attention which only two biological parents in a healthy relationship could bring. It is even more likely that it was easier for them to take their anger out on me because I was the outsider. Perhaps I just quit on them too soon out of frustration and fear. Perhaps I was beaten down by all the chaos and mayhem that ensued. I offer my deepest condolences to them. Perhaps they had no awareness of their contributions to my unhappiness as well. Because of that I forgive them.

When you grow up without the benefit of knowing your father because his life was taken by another individual, you can't help but feel a void that perhaps you're not even aware exits. Rasheed, Kashif, and Anne were victims of life's cruelties, too. It is possible that they suffered from some form of dysfunction while being exposed to everything that ensued. I thank God that they shared the better parts of me. They have compassion for others and a tenacious spirit. Perhaps they believe that I made some mistakes and failed them in some ways. It is even likely that one day they, too, may live out some of the dysfunctional behaviors they may have learned from me. It is plausible that they view my life as a lesson they dare not repeat. They realize that I'm not perfect but that I have been the best mother to them I could be. Perhaps they love me unconditionally. For that I'm grateful.

When you are forced to deal with another person's addictions, the possibility of having a pleasurable experience is slim to none. Rita never made things easy for me or even for herself when she was trapped in her addiction. When a person is beaten down and has lost everything they've come to know, how can we judge them? Drug and alcohol abuse are probably the worst forms of addictions because they affect more than just the addict. Unless you've lived at that address, it's hard to relate to the pain that individuals feel as they go through the process.

Perhaps Rita didn't understand the boundaries she crossed when she told Leah that she was her biological mother. It is possible that she can't even comprehend the deep scars that Leah endured from her actions. Perhaps Rita was hurting so bad that she, too, needed acceptance. Maybe Deon and I could have set aside our anger long enough to have shown her more compassion and support during her illness. It is possible that we could have made a difference. Rita is one of God's children. Because of that I forgive her.

Some people's relationships can't even last the 72 days that Kim Kardashian's marriage did. The commitment simply isn't there. In our society, the effort to make marriage work has been tossed by the wayside. Deon and I have been together for twenty years. That's worth bragging about in today's society. We masked a lot of our problems by avoiding them, which is common with relationships that go the distance. Avoidance can be detrimental to any relationship. Therefore, couples must keep the lines of communication open. Deon and I have always been best friends, but we allowed equal amounts of the other's dysfunction to nearly ruin our relationship. We can't blame our dysfunction on anyone else.

It is probable that Deon never had a positive male figure to model what parenting and family values looked like. It is even more plausible that men don't accept or realize that there is something wrong with them. It is likely that Deon suffered the same emotional scars as Marcus and Terry from his parent's abandonment. Perhaps Deon hides behind his outer appearance as a crutch for facing the world each day. It is possible that he, too, fears being alone and wants to do things differently than his parents did. Moreover, Deon is a man who deeply loves a woman as much as he loves himself. Because of that I have forgiven him.

CHAPTER 36

Released to Live Life Out Loud

Once I got tired of repeating the same behaviors, I was forced to analyze my own addiction to dysfunction. I never chose to have an addiction; most addicts don't. Addiction can happen to anyone. We have all experienced some sort of dysfunction in our lives. Dysfunction can be exhibited through various feelings and emotions: *Anger, Ego, Jealousy, Envy, Hate, and Lust* — you name it. As for me, my addiction manifested itself through channels of fear and anger. I did not realize that my responses to life's challenges were deeply rooted in fear. When I was afraid, I became angry, and when I was scared, I hid myself. That volatile recipe allowed the devil to seize the opportunity to take over my mind. When we establish a strong bond with God, there is no room for fear. His protection is everlasting. However, when we retreat and hide ourselves, our adversary welcomes us to a life we no longer recognize.

It is important to be aware that our exposure to dysfunction is interrelated to our propensity to act out certain behaviors in life. We are generally exposed to the dysfunctional behaviors of our parents and simply repeat the cycle in our own lives, and I just didn't have the wherewithal to break free from my addiction to dysfunction.

We really have to safeguard our mind, spirit, body, and soul by feeding it positive affirmations, prayers, and through a personal relationship with our Heavenly Father. We need Him to complete us. God gave us Jesus, and Jesus has the power to create a *"new"* you.

In many of my relationships, I reprioritized God's order and didn't give Him His rightful place. God got closer to the bottom of the list, whereas the men in my life held a place of higher significance. I made an egregious mistake and paid a substantial price. I have come to realize that I really need to speak to God daily and allow Him to shower me with the love I desire. There is no earthly man that can provide me with the love I need like God can.

It is 2012; I'm finding inner peace and learning to relinquish those things that have hampered my spiritual growth over the years. I've taken an honest inventory of my life, and God is placing everything in its proper perspective for me. I can see as though I am looking through a clear pair of lenses. If I'm being truthful, I love a lot of what I'm feeling and seeing. However, what I don't like is the part of me that I have allowed to erode while under the control of other people and things. Honest reflection is tough. It's similar to getting a grade of F on a paper on which you worked so hard. You thought you dotted all your I's and crossed all your T's, only to find out that you made a lot of technical errors in the process.

Facing my fears has been my first area of business to tackle. I'm learning that by facing them I am able to let go of the non-forgiveness that I've held on to for so long. I'm taking full responsibility for managing my life and creating balance. Learning to fall back in love with myself has been paramount to my healing. I will spend the rest of this year working on my overall self-health. It time for me to be the *confident woman* I was meant to be. God is rebirthing me and showing me that I am still his beautiful daffodil. It's my season; it's my time. I've had a burial service for the negative lessons: disappointment, choices, forgiveness, awareness, and acceptance. In fact, the only two individuals still alive are James, who came to teach *forgiveness,* and Deon, who came to teach *acceptance.* For me, those were the two hardest lessons to learn. They were the ones that caused me the most despair. I'm thankful that God showed me that throughout my life forgiveness and acceptance was the root cause for my addiction to dysfunction. God has been my helper along the way in both of these areas.

I'm turning disappointment into happiness, choices into freedom, forgiveness into appreciation, awareness into intuitiveness, and acceptance into love. I've gotten out of the boat, and I'm walking on water to a path that has led me to a rebirthing. I'm no longer *Addicted to Dysfunction*: I've been *Released: to Live Life Out Loud.*

www.ingramcontent.com/pod-product-compliance
Lightning Source LLC
Chambersburg PA
CBHW031545040426
42452CB00006B/188